At Issue

| Domestic Surveillance

Other Books in the At Issue Series:

At Issue

Domestic Surveillance

Tamara Thompson, Book Editor

GREENHAVEN PRESS
A part of Gale, Cengage Learning

GALE
CENGAGE Learning·

Farmington Hills, Mich • San Francisco • New York • Waterville, Maine
Meriden, Conn • Mason, Ohio • Chicago

Patricia Coryell, *Vice President & Publisher, New Products & GVRL*
Douglas Dentino, *Manager, New Products*
Judy Galens, *Acquisitions Editor*

For more information, contact:
Greenhaven Press
27500 Drake Rd.
Farmington Hills, MI 48331-3535
Or you can visit our Internet site at gale.cengage.com

For product information and technology assistance, contact us at

Gale Customer Support, 1-800-877-4253
For permission to use material from this text or product, submit all requests online at www.cengage.com/permissions

Further permissions questions can be emailed to permissionrequest@cengage.com

Articles in Greenhaven Press anthologies are often edited for length to meet page requirements. In addition, original titles of these works are changed to clearly present the main thesis and to explicitly indicate the author's opinion. Every effort is made to ensure that Greenhaven Press accurately reflects the original intent of the authors. Every effort has been made to trace the owners of copyrighted material.

Cover image © Todd Davidson/Illustration Works/Corbis.

LIBRARY OF CONGRESS CATALOGING-IN-PUBLICATION DATA

Domestic surveillance / Tamara Thompson, book editor.
    pages cm. -- (At issue)
   Includes bibliographical references and index.
   ISBN 978-0-7377-7163-3 (hardcover) -- ISBN 978-0-7377-7164-0 (pbk.)
   1. Espionage—United States. 2. Intelligence service—United States. I. Thompson, Tamara.
  JK468.I6D62 2015
  327.1273—dc23
                                2014026091

Contents

Introduction

When British author George Orwell depicted a dystopian future rife with surveillance by "Big Brother" in his book *1984*, written in 1948, little did he know it would become a common metaphor to discuss events unfolding in the United States more than sixty years later.

Domestic surveillance is big news these days because of a series of stunning revelations by Edward Snowden, a former National Security Agency (NSA) contractor who in 2013 exposed some of the country's most secret intelligence operations because he believed they are unconstitutional. The thirty-year-old computer specialist publicly released classified information about several key intelligence programs and then fled to Russia, where he gained temporary asylum and is still living.

Snowden's unprecedented leaks ignited a firestorm of controversy about the clandestine surveillance activities of US government agencies, particularly a secret mass electronic data-mining program by the NSA. Documents from Snowden revealed that at least since 2006 the NSA has been collecting— and archiving—nationwide electronic communications in bulk: e-mails, photos, videos, video and voice chats, voice-over-IP calls (such as Skype), details about file transfers and social networking, and more.

Snowden also revealed that the NSA had amassed an all-inclusive record of telephone metadata (data that describes other data), which includes numbers dialed, the duration of calls, and other details about phone usage in the United States over the past several years. The NSA legally compelled the nation's telecommunications companies to provide the information but forbid them from even acknowledging the program's existence.

The NSA maintains these operations are justified in the interest of national security under the USA PATRIOT Act, officially titled the Uniting and Strengthening America by Providing Appropriate Tools Required to Intercept and Obstruct Terrorism Act of 2001. This law, enacted after the 9/11 terrorist attacks, expanded the authority of intelligence agencies to gather and share information. The NSA also points out that its requests to access the communications information were approved by a special court established by the Foreign Intelligence Surveillance Act (FISA) of 1978. Section 215 of the USA PATRIOT Act further expanded the power of the FISA Act and its secret court.

According to the website of the Office of the Director of National Intelligence, a FISA court intelligence-gathering request "can only be used to obtain foreign intelligence information not concerning a United States person or to protect against international terrorism or clandestine intelligence activities. It cannot be used to investigate ordinary crimes, or even domestic terrorism."

Nevertheless, the NSA's electronic data-mining and phone metadata collection archives include information about millions of ordinary Americans who are not suspected of any wrongdoing. Privacy and civil rights advocates insist that such wholesale data gathering is an "electronic dragnet" that violates the Fourth Amendment of the US Constitution, which protects citizens from unreasonable search and seizure.

The intelligence community, meanwhile, is equally passionate in maintaining that Snowden's disclosures have badly compromised the United States' ability to conduct surveillance vital for national security and that ongoing access to such data is necessary to keep the country safe.

The NSA has defended its actions and has no intention of halting its activities. The most extensive surveillance of Americans ever conducted is ongoing, with some modifications ordered by President Barack Obama following intense public backlash when the scope of the program first became known. In April 2014, Obama ended the government's bulk retention of phone records in favor of having the records stored by a neutral third party, but he preserved the government's ability to continue accessing such data.

The matter is far from settled, however, with legal challenges winding their way through the courts, congressional committees holding hearings, and President Obama moving cautiously on the issue while promising to bring more transparency to what is still an overwhelmingly secretive process.

There is plenty of reason to be skeptical, critics say, based on the government's history of spying on its own citizens, and it's not the first time the NSA's actions have faced scrutiny. The NSA's illegal spying on Vietnam War opponents, including civil rights leader Dr. Martin Luther King Jr. and Senator Frank Church (who ultimately exposed the surveillance), led to the creation of FISA in the first place.

FISA was enacted to limit the powers of the NSA and it established the court that served as a functional process of judicial review for several decades. More recent interpretations of FISA under presidents George W. Bush and Obama, however, have granted far more leeway to intelligence agencies and have made the approval-court process even more secretive. The section of the PATRIOT Act that expanded FISA expires in 2015, and there is certain to be a fiery congressional debate about whether it should be continued in the interest of national security or scrapped on the basis of civil rights.

Although American founding father Benjamin Franklin is widely quoted as having said some version of the statement, "they who would give up essential liberty, to purchase a little temporary safety, deserve neither liberty nor safety," the conversation about domestic surveillance is no longer that clear-cut in today's high-tech world.

Even though events like September 11, 2001, or more recently the Boston Marathon bombings in 2013, influence people to welcome or accept increased domestic surveillance, the drive for better security is only one factor that contributes to the widespread monitoring of Americans.

While the government's intelligence programs are aggregating and analyzing staggering amounts of data, by and large they are not the ones actually gathering it. Ironically, the vast majority of information gathering is done not only with public consent but with its active participation. The technologies that make our lives safer, easier, and more connected also make Americans the most well-documented and most closely watched humans on the planet.

As Jonathan Schell notes in the September 2013 issue of the *Nation*, surveillance on such a massive scale "was impossible in the era of mere phone wiretapping, before the recent explosion of electronic communications—before the cellphones that disclose the whereabouts of their owners, the personal computers with their masses of personal data and easily penetrated defenses, the e-mails that flow through readily tapped cables and servers, the biometrics [devices that verify identity by confirming unique physical traits], the street-corner surveillance cameras. But now, to borrow the name of an intelligence program from the Bush years, 'Total Information Awareness' is technologically within reach."[1]

Eight months after Snowden blew the lid off the intelligence community's secrets, "the mind-boggling scope of the NSA's surveillance continues to make front-page news as a political story," writes media critic Norman Solomon in his February 2014 syndicated column. "But its most pernicious effects are social and psychological. We are getting accustomed

---

1. Jonathan Schell, "Edward Snowden and Chelsea Manning, the New Dissidents?" *The Nation*, September 4, 2013. http://www.thenation.com/article/176032/edward -snowden-and-chelsea-manning-new-dissidents#.

to Big Brother. Our daily lives are now accessible to prying eyes and ears no farther away than the nearest computer or cellphone."[2]

Who should—or should not—have access to the various types of information generated about Americans as they move through their daily lives is a key issue in the domestic surveillance controversy, and whether the practice of bulk data collection and analysis represents a threat to democracy or will ultimately prove to be its protector remains to be seen.

The authors in *At Issue: Domestic Surveillance* present a wide range of viewpoints about the extensive monitoring of American citizens and consider what the bulk collection of data might mean for both national security and democracy in the United States.

2. Norman Solomon, "Resisting the Surveillance State of Mind," Al Jazeera America, February 11, 2014. http://america.aljazeera.com/opinions/2014/2/nsa-surveillance privacycivilliberties.html.

1

Overview: What Is Domestic Surveillance?

Council on Foreign Relations

The Council on Foreign Relations is an independent, nonpartisan membership organization, think tank, and publishing house that helps policymakers and ordinary citizens alike better understand the world and the foreign policy choices facing the United States and other countries.

Following the terrorist attacks of September 11, 2001, the US government enacted a variety of regulations and programs to expand its intelligence-gathering efforts with the aim of strengthening national security and thwarting future attacks. The first and most well known, the USA PATRIOT Act, significantly expanded such activities and was the subject of much controversy, both at the time and since. Then-president George W. Bush also faced backlash over warrantless wire-tapping by the National Security Agency (NSA) in 2005. Eight years later, leaks of classified information by former NSA contractor Edward Snowden reignited the controversy over domestic surveillance when he exposed an extensive NSA data-gathering operation that secretly monitored the phone and Internet communications of millions of ordinary Americans.

In the wake of the September 11 [2001] attacks, Congress passed sweeping legislation to bolster U.S. counterterrorism efforts. Some of the most controversial measures, including

"Backgrounder: U.S. Domestic Surveillance," CFR.org, December 18, 2013. Reproduced by permission.

the 2001 USA PATRIOT Act [officially titled the Uniting and Strengthening America by Providing Appropriate Tools Required to Intercept and Obstruct Terrorism Act of 2001], significantly enhanced the federal government's ability to collect and analyze private information related to U.S. citizens. Proponents argue that the broader surveillance authorities are required to uncover and neutralize terrorism plots, while critics say the expanded powers infringe on civil liberties.

In 2005, the [George W.] Bush administration came under fire from Democrats and activist groups after press reports disclosed the National Security Agency's [NSA] warrantless wiretapping program. In 2013, the [Barack] Obama administration similarly attracted criticism from watchdog groups upon leaks related to its far-reaching domestic surveillance activities under the NSA. The episode has revived debate over privacy and national security and raised calls for reform.

Two NSA surveillance programs were exposed in press reports in June 2013. First, a *Guardian* report disclosed a classified Foreign Intelligence Surveillance Court (FISC) order instructing Verizon, one of the largest U.S. telecommunications firms, to hand over phone records of millions of Americans to the NSA. Another secret program, code-named PRISM, accessed troves of communication data—audio/video chats, emails, photos, and other media—from several U.S. technology companies, according to the *Washington Post*. Subsequent leaks revealed details on additional programs that gave the NSA extensive electronic surveillance tools, both domestic and international, allowing the government to track and tap into conversations of suspected terrorists, civilians, and even friendly foreign heads of state.

Obama Initially Defended the Program

Amid criticism from civil rights groups, the Obama administration initially defended the surveillance program, saying it is legal, limited, and effective in preventing terrorist attacks. Director of National Intelligence [DNI] James Clapper said the program does not monitor phone calls, but acquires telephony metadata to be queried only when there is a "reasonable suspicion" of links to a foreign terrorist organization.

After 9/11, the Bush administration opted not to seek approval from the FISC before intercepting "international communications into and out of the United States of persons linked to al-Qaeda or related terrorist organizations."

Experts say the White House is likely relying on Section 215 of the Patriot Act, a provision that says government can mandate the turnover of "any tangible things" from any entity as long as the items are for an investigation to defend against international terrorism or spying. In congressional testimony, NSA chief Gen. Keith Alexander credited his agency's surveillance with helping prevent "dozens" of terrorist attacks, and said he welcomed a debate on the legality of the programs.

In August [2013], President Obama created a task force of intelligence and legal experts to review NSA operations and recommend potential reforms. The inquiry is reportedly part of a comprehensive White House review of signals intelligence.

What Was the Domestic Surveillance Controversy Under Bush?

After 9/11, the Bush administration opted not to seek approval from the FISC before intercepting "international communications into and out of the United States of persons linked to al-Qaeda or related terrorist organizations." The special secret court, set up in 1978 following previous administrations' domestic spying abuses, was designed to act as a neutral overseer in granting government agencies surveillance authorization.

After the NSA program was revealed by the *New York Times* in late 2005, former attorney general Alberto R. Gonzales argued that President Bush had the legal authority under the constitution and congressional statute to conduct warrantless surveillance on U.S. persons "reasonably believed to be linked to al-Qaeda." The 2001 Authorization for Use of Military Force (AUMF), without specifically mentioning wiretapping, grants the president broad authority to use all necessary force "against those nations, organizations, or persons he determines planned, authorized, committed, or aided the [9/11] terrorist attacks." This includes, administration officials say, the powers to secretly gather domestic intelligence on al-Qaeda and associated groups.

The Bush administration maintained that the Foreign Intelligence Surveillance Act (FISA) was an outdated law-enforcement mechanism that was too time-consuming given the highly fluid, modern threat environment. Administration officials portrayed the NSA program as an "early warning system" with "a military nature that requires speed and agility." Moreover, the White House stressed that the program was one not of domestic surveillance but of monitoring terrorists abroad, and publicly referred to the operation as the "Terrorist Surveillance Program." Opponents of the program referred to it as "domestic spying."

President Obama reauthorized [the FISA Amendment Act] for five more years in December 2012.

Questions of Legality Lingered

Under congressional pressure, Gonzales announced in January 2007 plans to disband the warrantless surveillance program and cede oversight to FISC, but questions about the legality of the program lingered in Congress and Gonzales resigned months later.

But Washington's vow to seek FISA approval for domestic surveillance was short-lived. In July 2007—weeks before Gonzales stepped down—intelligence officials pressed lawmakers for emergency legislation to broaden their wiretapping authority following a ruling by the court overseeing FISA that impacted the government's ability to intercept foreign communications passing through telecommunications "switches" on U.S. soil.

In August, President Bush signed the Protect America Act of 2007, which gave the attorney general and the director of national intelligence temporary power to approve international surveillance, rather than the special intelligence court. It also said warrants are unnecessary for surveillance of a person "reasonably believed" to be located overseas. This six-month stopgap measure expired in early 2008, but the FISA Amendment Act passed just months later contained similar provisions. President Obama reauthorized this legislation for five more years in December 2012.

Why Did This Become an Issue in Mid-2013?

Edward Snowden, the ex-CIA [Central Intelligence Agency] and former NSA contractor who leaked news of the two NSA programs, cited concerns over civil liberties violations as his primary motive. "The NSA has built an infrastructure that allows it to intercept almost everything. With this capability, the vast majority of human communications are automatically ingested without targeting. If I wanted to see your emails or your wife's phone, all I have to do is use intercepts. I can get your emails, passwords, phone records, credit cards," he said in an interview with the *Guardian*.

However, DNI Director Clapper publicly denied initial media reports that the PRISM surveillance program was "an undisclosed collection or data mining program" that unilaterally taps into servers of U.S. telecoms. Rather, he stated the

NSA program was limited and had been "widely known and publicly discussed since its inception in 2008." Specifically, Clapper said the program operated under Section 702 of FISA that permits the targeting of non-U.S. persons abroad without individualized court orders. As noted above, President Obama has reauthorized this legislation until 2017.

Many U.S. lawmakers have pressed for Snowden's prosecution, and the Obama administration referred his case to the Justice Department. Snowden fled to Hong Kong in May [2013] and was granted temporary asylum in Russia in August after spending weeks at the Moscow airport.

What Are the Challenges to Domestic Surveillance Policy?

Both Democratic and Republican lawmakers have called for a reexamination of the government's broad surveillance powers in the wake of disclosures regarding NSA activities. Top-ranking Senators Dianne Feinstein (D-CA) and John McCain (R-AZ) supported requests for congressional hearings on NSA surveillance, despite their support for the controversial programs. Sen. Ron Wyden (D-OR), an outspoken critic of NSA's broad authorities, has called on the White House to detail the extent to which Americans were monitored. In the past, the NSA said it lacked the technical ability to quantify this data.

Legal analysts say that while the [Obama] recommendations, if implemented, would require greater executive, congressional, and judicial review of surveillance activities, they would end few programs.

Critics allege that even if the programs are operating within the letter of law, as the Obama administration says, they violate the law's intent and the values of democratic society. Some civil liberties activists have appealed for a thorough review of several provisions in the Patriot Act and FISA Amendments Act that provide controversial surveillance authorities.

Civil libertarians question whether government surveillance programs violate the Fourth Amendment to the U.S. Constitution, which states: "The right of the people to be secure in their persons, houses, papers, and effects, against unreasonable searches and seizures, shall not be violated, and no Warrants shall issue, but upon probable cause, supported by Oath or affirmation, and particularly describing the place to be searched, and the persons or things to be seized."

Legal Challenges

In December [2013], Judge Richard J. Leon of the Federal District Court for the District of Columbia ruled that the NSA's bulk gathering of U.S. telephone metadata likely violates the Constitution. "Surely, such a program infringes on 'that degree of privacy' that the founders enshrined in the Fourth Amendment," he wrote. The judge ordered the government to stop collecting data on calls of the two plaintiffs in the case, but stayed the injunction to allow the government a chance to appeal. Other legal challenges are in early phases, including suits by the American Civil Liberties Union and the Electronic Frontier Foundation.

The Obama administration's task force also released its findings in December, recommending dozens of changes to current surveillance practice. Significant proposed reforms include: ending the government's indiscrimate collection of U.S. telephone metadata and requiring authorities to obtain a court order to query this information, held in the private sector; placing new limits on the monitoring of foreign leaders and ordinary non-Americans; and supporting new encryption standards and technologies. But legal analysts say that while the recommendations, if implemented, would require greater executive, congressional, and judicial review of surveillance activities, they would end few programs.

Meanwhile, in Congress, two bills that would forbid the NSA from collecting phone data on Americans not suspected of a crime are still in the early legislative process. The USA Freedom Act, which would reform the Patriot Act to address privacy concerns, has enough support to pass, but lawmakers are uncertain when it will be ready for a vote. Still, many Democrats and Republicans say the NSA programs are essential counterterrorism tools that have proved effective in preventing potential attacks.

2

The National Security Agency Violates Civil Rights

Ted Lieu and Joel Anderson

Ted Lieu and Joel Anderson are state senators in California.

Whether or not a particular government program might be effective is of little importance if a key question is not answered first: whether the program itself is constitutional. The National Security Agency (NSA) has failed to pass constitutional muster and has been violating the Fourth Amendment by collecting communications information from millions of ordinary Americans without either a warrant or any sort of probable cause. Not only is this nationwide information dragnet unconstitutional, there is little evidence that it has even been effective. President Barack Obama should rein in the NSA and other US intelligence agencies and remind them that their primary allegiance is to uphold the US Constitution, not to the unbridled pursuit of the data they are gathering.

Few people would quarrel with the view that the president's primary duty is to protect and defend the United States. But that is not what the U.S. Constitution actually says. Article Two, Section One, Clause Eight of the Constitution states that before the president can take office, he must take an oath to "preserve, protect and defend the Constitution of the United States."

Ted Lieu and Joel Anderson, "NSA's Bulk Data Collection Program Unconstitutional: Ted Lieu and Joel Anderson," *Torrance Daily Breeze* online, January 16, 2014. www.daily breeze.com. Reproduced by permission.

This is not just a technicality. Under our constitutional republic, the first question to ask of any federal program is not whether it might be effective. The first question is whether the program is constitutional. If the program violates the Constitution, then the executive branch cannot implement the program. Our founders enacted the Bill of Rights because they understood the dangers of unchecked governmental power.

For years, the National Security Agency [NSA] has been violating the Fourth Amendment rights of all 317 million Americans, including more than 38 million Californians, through its searches and seizures of our phone and other electronic records. The NSA knows what phone numbers you dialed, who called you, when the calls were made and the duration of the calls. Media investigations have revealed the NSA has also collected vast amounts of electronic data, including emails, text messages and other internet traffic.

Not only is the NSA's massive dragnet unconstitutional, the NSA has produced little to no evidence that the program has been effective.

The Fourth Amendment

The Fourth Amendment is straightforward: "The right of the people to be secure in their persons, houses, papers, and effects, against unreasonable searches and seizures, shall not be violated, and no Warrants shall issue, but upon probable cause, supported by Oath or affirmation, and particularly describing the place to be searched, and the persons or things to be seized."

The only way the NSA—or any other governmental agency—can seize your private information is by a specific warrant issued by a judge based on probable cause. The NSA has failed to secure individualized warrants against all Americans. That's because it can't. Americans do not become reasonably suspicious simply for making and receiving phone calls.

Not only is the NSA's massive dragnet unconstitutional, the NSA has produced little to no evidence that the program has been effective.

In response to the NSA's mass violations of our civil liberties, last week [January 2014] we introduced Senate Bill 828 as an emergency measure, meaning it would take effect immediately once signed into law. This bipartisan legislation would prohibit state agencies and officials from providing material support to the NSA unless a specific warrant has issued. Titled the Fourth Amendment Protection Act, similar legislation also has been introduced in Arizona and recently replicated in Oklahoma. Several other states are considering similar legislation.

Significant Reforms Are Needed

At a minimum, the president needs to stop the NSA's unconstitutional bulk data seizure program. He also needs to reform the Foreign Intelligence Surveillance Court, a secret star-chamber process in which judges only hear arguments made by the NSA.

To restore confidence in our nation's intelligence agencies, the president should issue a directive instructing intelligence officials that their first allegiance is to the Constitution. He should also remove or at least discipline the director of National Intelligence, James Clapper, Jr., who lied to Congress last March [2013] by denying the NSA collected data on millions of Americans. Our democracy cannot function if intelligence officials believe they have free reign to lie to the public.

As the president considers what reforms to make, we hope he keeps in mind that the last time our federal government violated the Constitution on a mass basis in the name of national security, more than 100,000 Americans were rounded up and interned.

3

The National Security Agency Is Acting Within the Law

James R. Clapper

James R. Clapper is the director of national intelligence for the United States.

The tools, techniques, and programs used by American intelligence-gathering agencies are most effective when they are secret, so the illegal public disclosure of such information has been very damaging to intelligence operations in the United States. The National Security Agency's collection of telephone and other communication data has been done entirely within the law; Americans are not being spied upon. The country's various intelligence programs operate with strict oversight and accountability, and those who work in such agencies are committed to protecting the privacy and civil liberties of all Americans. To reassure the public, the Office of the Director of National Intelligence will continue to declassify documents related to intelligence activities whenever possible.

Thanks so much for having us here today, to talk about the way ahead, occasioned by the continuing dramatic revelations about intelligence collection programs since their unauthorized disclosure.

And about the steps we're taking to make these programs more transparent, while still protecting our national security interests. . . .

James R. Clapper, "Remarks as Delivered by James R. Clapper, Director of National Intelligence, Open Hearing on Continued Oversight of the Foreign Intelligence Surveillance Act to the House Permanent Select Committee on Intelligence," *IC On The Record*, October 29, 2013. www.icontherecord.tumblr.com.

This hearing is a key part of the discussion our nation needs, about legislation that provides the Intelligence Community with authorities, both to collect critical foreign intelligence, and to protect privacy and civil liberties.

We—all of us—in the Intelligence Community, are very much aware that the recent unauthorized disclosures have raised serious concerns that you alluded to, both here in Congress, and across the nation, about our intelligence activities.

We know the public wants to understand how its Intelligence Community uses its special tools and authorities, and to judge whether we can be trusted to use them appropriately. We believe we have been lawful, and that the rigorous oversight we've operated under has been effective. So we welcome this opportunity to make our case to the public.

In the last few months, the manner in which our activities have been characterized has often been incomplete, inaccurate, or misleading, or some combination thereof.

Revelations Have Been Damaging

As we engage in this discussion, I think it's also important that our citizens know that the unauthorized disclosure of the details of these programs has been extremely damaging. From my vantage, as DNI [Director of National Intelligence], these disclosures are threatening our ability to conduct intelligence, and to keep our country safe. There's no way to erase, or make up for, the damage that we know has already been done, and we anticipate even more, as we continue our assessment— and as more revelations are made.

Before these unauthorized disclosures, we were always very conservative about discussing the specifics of our collection programs, based on the truism that the more adversaries know about what we're doing, the more they can avoid our surveillance. But the disclosures, for better or for worse, have lowered the threshold for discussing these matters in public. So, to the degree that we can discuss them, we will.

But this public discussion should be based on an accurate understanding of the Intelligence Community: Who we are, what we do, and how we're overseen.

In the last few months, the manner in which our activities have been characterized has often been incomplete, inaccurate, or misleading, or some combination thereof.

I believe that most Americans realize the Intelligence Community exists to collect the vital intelligence that helps protect our nation from foreign threats. We focus on uncovering the secret plans and intentions of our foreign adversaries, as we've been charged to do.

But what we do not do is spy unlawfully on Americans, or for that matter, spy indiscriminately on the citizens of any country. We only "spy" for valid foreign intelligence purposes, as authorized by law, with multiple layers of oversight, to ensure we don't abuse our authorities.

Keeping the Public Trust

Unfortunately, this reality has sometimes been obscured in the current debate. And for some, this has led to an erosion of trust in the Intelligence Community.

And we do understand the concerns on the part of the public. I'm a Vietnam veteran, and I remember, as Congressional investigations of the 1970s later disclosed—and I was in the Intelligence Community then—that some intelligence programs were carried out for domestic political purposes, without proper legal authorization or oversight.

But having lived through that, as a part of the Intelligence Community, I can now assure the American people that the Intelligence Community of today is not like that. We operate within a robust framework of strict rules and rigorous oversight, involving all three branches of the government.

Another useful historical perspective, I think, is that during the Cold War, the Free World and the Soviet bloc had mutually exclusive telecommunications systems, which made foreign collection a lot easier to distinguish.

If we had an alarm bell that went off whenever one terrorist communicated with another terrorist, our jobs would be infinitely easier. But that capability just doesn't exist in the world of technology.

Now, world telecommunications are unified. Intertwined with hundreds of millions of innocent people, conducting billions of innocent transactions, are a much smaller number of nefarious adversaries who are trying to do harm on the very same network, using the very same technologies. So, our challenge is to distinguish, very precisely, between these two groups of communicants.

If we had an alarm bell that went off whenever one terrorist communicated with another terrorist, our jobs would be infinitely easier. But that capability just doesn't exist in the world of technology, at least today.

Documents Are Being Declassified

Over the past months, I've declassified and publicly released a series of documents related to both Section 215 of the PATRIOT Act [The USA PATRIOT Act, officially titled the Uniting and Strengthening America by Providing Appropriate Tools Required to Intercept and Obstruct Terrorism Act of 2001] and Section 702 of the Foreign Intelligence Surveillance Act, or FISA.

We're doing that to facilitate informed public debate about the important intelligence collection programs that operate under these authorities. We felt that in light of the unauthorized disclosures, the public interest in these documents far outweighed the potential additional damage to national security.

These documents let our citizens see the seriousness, the thoroughness, and the rigor with which the FISA Court exercises its responsibilities. They also reflect the Intelligence Community's—particularly NSA's [National Security Agency]—commitment to uncovering, reporting, and correcting any compliance matters that occur. However, even in these documents, we've had to redact certain information to protect sensitive sources and methods, such as particular targets of surveillance.

But we will continue to declassify more documents. That's what the American people want, it's what the President has asked us to do, and I personally believe it's the only way we can reassure our citizens that their Intelligence Community [IC] is using its tools and authorities appropriately.

The rules and oversight that govern us ensure we do what the American people want us to do, which is protect our nation's security and our people's liberties.

We in the IC stand ready to work in partnership with you, to adjust foreign surveillance authorities, to further protect our privacy and civil liberties.

So I'll repeat: We do not spy on anyone except for valid foreign intelligence purposes, and we only work within the law. Now to be sure, on occasion, we've made mistakes—some quite significant. But these are usually caused by human error or technical problems. And whenever we've found mistakes, we've reported, addressed, and corrected them.

The National Security Agency specifically, as part of the Intelligence Community broadly, is an honorable institution. The men and women who do this sensitive work are honorable people, dedicated to conducting their mission lawfully, and are appalled by any wrongdoing. They, too, are citizens of this nation, who care just as much about privacy and constitutional rights as the rest of us. They should be commended for their crucial and important work in protecting the people of this country, which has been made all the more difficult by the torrent of unauthorized, damaging disclosures.

Principles to Agree On

That all said, we in the IC stand ready to work in partnership with you, to adjust foreign surveillance authorities, to further protect our privacy and civil liberties. And I think there are some principles we already agree on.

First, we must always protect our sources, methods, targets, partners, and liaison relationships.

[Second,] we must do a better job in helping the American people understand what we do, why we do it, and, most importantly, the rigorous oversight that helps ensure we do it correctly.

And third, we must take every opportunity to demonstrate our commitment to respecting the civil liberties and privacy of every American.

But, we also have to remain mindful of the potential negative long-term impact of over-correcting the authorizations granted to the Intelligence Community. As Americans, we face an unending array of threats to our way of life, more than I've seen in my 50 years in intelligence. And we need to sustain our ability to detect these threats.

We certainly welcome a balanced discussion about national security and civil liberties. It's not an either/or situation; we need to continue to protect both.

4

The United States Must Balance Security and Privacy Needs

Barack Obama

Barack Obama is the forty-fourth president of the United States.

In response to public backlash about domestic surveillance following the disclosure that the National Security Agency (NSA) collects the phone records of millions of Americans, President Barack Obama delivered a speech in which he spoke of the history and effectiveness of surveillance and intelligence-gathering programs and the need to balance them with the deeply held American values of freedom and privacy. Toward that end, Obama set forth a series of new oversights and reforms to act as checks and balances on the American security apparatus. The president believes that "more robust public discussion about the balance between security and liberty" is necessary and good for the country.

At the dawn of our Republic, a small, secret surveillance committee borne out of the "The Sons of Liberty" was established in Boston. And the group's members included Paul Revere. At night, they would patrol the streets, reporting back any signs that the British were preparing raids against America's early Patriots.

Throughout American history, intelligence has helped secure our country and our freedoms. In the Civil War, Union

Barack Obama, "Speech on Changes to National Security Agency Programs, US Justice Department," The White House, January 17, 2014. www.whitehouse.gov.

balloon reconnaissance tracked the size of Confederate armies by counting the number of campfires. In World War II, code-breakers gave us insights into Japanese war plans, and when [General George S.] Patton marched across Europe, intercepted communications helped save the lives of his troops. After the war, the rise of the Iron Curtain and nuclear weapons only increased the need for sustained intelligence gathering. And so, in the early days of the Cold War, President [Harry S.] Truman created the National Security Agency, or NSA, to give us insights into the Soviet bloc, and provide our leaders with information they needed to confront aggression and avert catastrophe.

Lessons from History

Throughout this evolution, we benefited from both our Constitution and our traditions of limited government. U.S. intelligence agencies were anchored in a system of checks and balances—with oversight from elected leaders, and protections for ordinary citizens. Meanwhile, totalitarian states like East Germany offered a cautionary tale of what could happen when vast, unchecked surveillance turned citizens into informers, and persecuted people for what they said in the privacy of their own homes.

It is hard to overstate the transformation America's intelligence community had to go through after 9/11.

In fact, even the United States proved not to be immune to the abuse of surveillance. And in the 1960s, government spied on civil rights leaders and critics of the Vietnam War. And partly in response to these revelations, additional laws were established in the 1970s to ensure that our intelligence capabilities could not be misused against our citizens. In the long, twilight struggle against Communism, we had been reminded that the very liberties that we sought to preserve could not be sacrificed at the altar of national security.

The Modern World

If the fall of the Soviet Union left America without a competing superpower, emerging threats from terrorist groups, and the proliferation of weapons of mass destruction placed new and in some ways more complicated demands on our intelligence agencies. Globalization and the Internet made these threats more acute, as technology erased borders and empowered individuals to project great violence, as well as great good. Moreover, these new threats raised new legal and new policy questions. For while few doubted the legitimacy of spying on hostile states, our framework of laws was not fully adapted to prevent terrorist attacks by individuals acting on their own, or acting in small, ideologically driven groups on behalf of a foreign power.

The horror of September 11th [2001] brought all these issues to the fore. Across the political spectrum, Americans recognized that we had to adapt to a world in which a bomb could be built in a basement, and our electric grid could be shut down by operators an ocean away. We were shaken by the signs we had missed leading up to the attacks—how the hijackers had made phone calls to known extremists and traveled to suspicious places. So we demanded that our intelligence community improve its capabilities, and that law enforcement change practices to focus more on preventing attacks before they happen than prosecuting terrorists after an attack.

It is hard to overstate the transformation America's intelligence community had to go through after 9/11. Our agencies suddenly needed to do far more than the traditional mission of monitoring hostile powers and gathering information for policymakers. Instead, they were now asked to identify and target plotters in some of the most remote parts of the world, and to anticipate the actions of networks that, by their very nature, cannot be easily penetrated with spies or informants. . . .

In the Name of National Security

In our rush to respond to a very real and novel set of threats, the risk of government overreach—the possibility that we lose some of our core liberties in pursuit of security—also became more pronounced. We saw, in the immediate aftermath of 9/11, our government engaged in enhanced interrogation techniques that contradicted our values. As a Senator, I was critical of several practices, such as warrantless wiretaps. And all too often new authorities were instituted without adequate public debate.

Through a combination of action by the courts, increased congressional oversight, and adjustments by the previous administration, some of the worst excesses that emerged after 9/11 were curbed by the time I took office. But a variety of factors have continued to complicate America's efforts to both defend our nation and uphold our civil liberties.

America's capabilities are unique, and the power of new technologies means that there are fewer and fewer technical constraints on what we can do.

First, the same technological advances that allow U.S. intelligence agencies to pinpoint an al Qaeda cell in Yemen or an email between two terrorists in the Sahel also mean that many routine communications around the world are within our reach. And at a time when more and more of our lives are digital, that prospect is disquieting for all of us.

Second, the combination of increased digital information and powerful supercomputers offers intelligence agencies the possibility of sifting through massive amounts of bulk data to identify patterns or pursue leads that may thwart impending threats. It's a powerful tool. But the government collection and storage of such bulk data also creates a potential for abuse.

Rules for Foreigners Are Different

Third, the legal safeguards that restrict surveillance against U.S. persons without a warrant do not apply to foreign persons overseas. This is not unique to America; few, if any, spy agencies around the world constrain their activities beyond their own borders. And the whole point of intelligence is to obtain information that is not publicly available. But America's capabilities are unique, and the power of new technologies means that there are fewer and fewer technical constraints on what we can do. That places a special obligation on us to ask tough questions about what we should do.

And finally, intelligence agencies cannot function without secrecy, which makes their work less subject to public debate. Yet there is an inevitable bias not only within the intelligence community, but among all of us who are responsible for national security, to collect more information about the world, not less. So in the absence of institutional requirements for regular debate—and oversight that is public, as well as private or classified—the danger of government overreach becomes more acute. And this is particularly true when surveillance technology and our reliance on digital information is evolving much faster than our laws.

For all these reasons, I maintained a healthy skepticism toward our surveillance programs after I became President. I ordered that our programs be reviewed by my national security team and our lawyers, and in some cases I ordered changes in how we did business. We increased oversight and auditing, including new structures aimed at compliance. Improved rules were proposed by the government and approved by the Foreign Intelligence Surveillance Court. And we sought to keep Congress continually updated on these activities.

What I did not do is stop these programs wholesale—not only because I felt that they made us more secure, but also because nothing in that initial review, and nothing that I have learned since, indicated that our intelligence community has sought to violate the law or is cavalier about the civil liberties of their fellow citizens.

For our intelligence community to be effective over the long haul, we must maintain the trust of the American people, and people around the world.

Wielding Authority Wisely

To the contrary, in an extraordinarily difficult job—one in which actions are second-guessed, success is unreported, and failure can be catastrophic—the men and women of the intelligence community, including the NSA, consistently follow protocols designed to protect the privacy of ordinary people. They're not abusing authorities in order to listen to your private phone calls or read your emails. When mistakes are made—which is inevitable in any large and complicated human enterprise—they correct those mistakes. Laboring in obscurity, often unable to discuss their work even with family and friends, the men and women at the NSA know that if another 9/11 or massive cyber-attack occurs, they will be asked, by Congress and the media, why they failed to connect the dots. What sustains those who work at NSA and our other intelligence agencies through all these pressures is the knowledge that their professionalism and dedication play a central role in the defense of our nation.

Now, to say that our intelligence community follows the law, and is staffed by patriots, is not to suggest that I or others in my administration felt complacent about the potential impact of these programs. Those of us who hold office in America have a responsibility to our Constitution, and while I was confident in the integrity of those who lead our intelligence community, it was clear to me in observing our intelligence operations on a regular basis that changes in our technological capabilities were raising new questions about the privacy safeguards currently in place.

More Review and Discussion Are Needed

Moreover, after an extended review of our use of drones in the fight against terrorist networks, I believed a fresh examination of our surveillance programs was a necessary next step in our effort to get off the open-ended war footing that we've maintained since 9/11. And for these reasons, I indicated in a speech at the National Defense University last May [2013] that we needed a more robust public discussion about the balance between security and liberty. Of course, what I did not know at the time is that within weeks of my speech, an avalanche of unauthorized disclosures would spark controversies at home and abroad that have continued to this day. . . .

We have to make some important decisions about how to protect ourselves and sustain our leadership in the world, while upholding the civil liberties and privacy protections that our ideals and our Constitution require. We need to do so not only because it is right, but because the challenges posed by threats like terrorism and proliferation and cyber-attacks are not going away any time soon. They are going to continue to be a major problem. And for our intelligence community to be effective over the long haul, we must maintain the trust of the American people, and people around the world.

This effort will not be completed overnight, and given the pace of technological change, we shouldn't expect this to be the last time America has this debate. But I want the American people to know that the work has begun. Over the last six months, I created an outside Review Group on Intelligence and Communications Technologies to make recommendations for reform. I consulted with the Privacy and Civil Liberties

Oversight Board, created by Congress. I've listened to foreign partners, privacy advocates, and industry leaders. My administration has spent countless hours considering how to approach intelligence in this era of diffuse threats and technological revolution. . . .

Those who are troubled by our existing programs are not interested in repeating the tragedy of 9/11, and those who defend these programs are not dismissive of civil liberties.

Just as ardent civil libertarians recognize the need for robust intelligence capabilities, those with responsibilities for our national security readily acknowledge the potential for abuse as intelligence capabilities advance and more and more private information is digitized. After all, the folks at NSA and other intelligence agencies are our neighbors. They're our friends and family. They've got electronic bank and medical records like everybody else. They have kids on Facebook and Instagram, and they know, more than most of us, the vulnerabilities to privacy that exist in a world where transactions are recorded, and emails and text and messages are stored, and even our movements can increasingly be tracked through the GPS [global positioning system] on our phones. . . .

A Higher Standard

All of us understand that the standards for government surveillance must be higher. Given the unique power of the state, it is not enough for leaders to say: Trust us, we won't abuse the data we collect. For history has too many examples when that trust has been breached. Our system of government is built on the premise that our liberty cannot depend on the good intentions of those in power; it depends on the law to constrain those in power.

I make these observations to underscore that the basic values of most Americans when it comes to questions of surveillance and privacy converge a lot more than the crude characterizations that have emerged over the last several months. Those who are troubled by our existing programs are not interested in repeating the tragedy of 9/11, and those who defend these programs are not dismissive of civil liberties.

The challenge is getting the details right, and that is not simple. In fact, during the course of our review, I have often reminded myself I would not be where I am today were it not for the courage of dissidents like Dr. [Martin Luther] King [Jr.], who were spied upon by their own government. And as President, a President who looks at intelligence every morning, I also can't help but be reminded that America must be vigilant in the face of threats.

Fortunately, by focusing on facts and specifics rather than speculation and hypotheticals, this review process has given me—and hopefully the American people—some clear direction for change. And today, I can announce a series of concrete and substantial reforms that my administration intends to adopt administratively or will seek to codify with Congress.

We can and should be more transparent in how government uses [its] authority.

Proposed Reforms

First, I have approved a new presidential directive for our signals intelligence activities both at home and abroad. This guidance will strengthen executive branch oversight of our intelligence activities. It will ensure that we take into account our security requirements, but also our alliances; our trade and investment relationships, including the concerns of American companies; and our commitment to privacy and basic liberties. And we will review decisions about intelligence priorities and sensitive targets on an annual basis so that our actions are regularly scrutinized by my senior national security team.

Second, we will reform programs and procedures in place to provide greater transparency to our surveillance activities, and fortify the safeguards that protect the privacy of U.S. persons. Since we began this review, including information being released today, we have declassified over 40 opinions and orders of the Foreign Intelligence Surveillance Court, which provides judicial review of some of our most sensitive intelligence activities—including the Section 702 program targeting foreign individuals overseas, and the Section 215 telephone metadata program.

And going forward, I'm directing the Director of National Intelligence, in consultation with the Attorney General, to annually review for the purposes of declassification any future opinions of the court with broad privacy implications, and to report to me and to Congress on these efforts. To ensure that the court hears a broader range of privacy perspectives, I am also calling on Congress to authorize the establishment of a panel of advocates from outside government to provide an independent voice in significant cases before the Foreign Intelligence Surveillance Court. . . .

Scrutiny of National Security Letters

In investigating threats, the FBI [Federal Bureau of Investigation] also relies on what's called national security letters, which can require companies to provide specific and limited information to the government without disclosing the orders to the subject of the investigation. These are cases in which it's important that the subject of the investigation, such as a possible terrorist or spy, isn't tipped off. But we can and should be more transparent in how government uses this authority.

I have therefore directed the Attorney General to amend how we use national security letters so that this secrecy will not be indefinite, so that it will terminate within a fixed time unless the government demonstrates a real need for further secrecy. We will also enable communications providers to make public more information than ever before about the orders that they have received to provide data to the government.

This brings me to the program that has generated the most controversy these past few months—the bulk collection of telephone records under Section 215. Let me repeat what I said when this story first broke: This program does not involve the content of phone calls, or the names of people making calls. Instead, it provides a record of phone numbers and the times and lengths of calls—metadata that can be queried if and when we have a reasonable suspicion that a particular number is linked to a terrorist organization.

I believe critics are right to point out that without proper safeguards, this type of program could be used to yield more information about our private lives, and open the door to more intrusive bulk collection programs in the future.

Why is this necessary? The program grew out of a desire to address a gap identified after 9/11. One of the 9/11 hijackers—Khalid al-Mihdhar—made a phone call from San Diego to a known al Qaeda safe-house in Yemen. NSA saw that call, but it could not see that the call was coming from an individual already in the United States. The telephone metadata program under Section 215 was designed to map the communications of terrorists so we can see who they may be in contact with as quickly as possible. And this capability could also prove valuable in a crisis. For example, if a bomb goes off in one of our cities and law enforcement is racing to determine whether a network is poised to conduct additional attacks, time is of the essence. Being able to quickly review phone connections to assess whether a network exists is critical to that effort.

Phone Program Is Essential

In sum, the program does not involve the NSA examining the phone records of ordinary Americans. Rather, it consolidates these records into a database that the government can query if it has a specific lead—a consolidation of phone records that the companies already retained for business purposes. The review group turned up no indication that this database has been intentionally abused. And I believe it is important that the capability that this program is designed to meet is preserved.

Having said that, I believe critics are right to point out that without proper safeguards, this type of program could be used to yield more information about our private lives, and open the door to more intrusive bulk collection programs in the future. They're also right to point out that although the telephone bulk collection program was subject to oversight by the Foreign Intelligence Surveillance Court and has been reauthorized repeatedly by Congress, it has never been subject to vigorous public debate.

For all these reasons, I believe we need a new approach. I am therefore ordering a transition that will end the Section 215 bulk metadata program as it currently exists, and establish a mechanism that preserves the capabilities we need without the government holding this bulk metadata.

This will not be simple. The review group recommended that our current approach be replaced by one in which the providers or a third party retain the bulk records, with government accessing information as needed. Both of these options pose difficult problems. Relying solely on the records of multiple providers, for example, could require companies to alter their procedures in ways that raise new privacy concerns.

On the other hand, any third party maintaining a single, consolidated database would be carrying out what is essentially a government function but with more expense, more legal ambiguity, potentially less accountability—all of which would have a doubtful impact on increasing public confidence that their privacy is being protected. . . .

When you cut through the noise, what's really at stake is how we remain true to who we are in a world that is remaking itself at dizzying speed.

Balancing Security and Privacy

The reforms I'm proposing today should give the American people greater confidence that their rights are being protected, even as our intelligence and law enforcement agencies maintain the tools they need to keep us safe. And I recognize that there are additional issues that require further debate. For example, some who participated in our review, as well as some members of Congress, would like to see more sweeping reforms to the use of national security letters so that we have to go to a judge each time before issuing these requests. . . .

There are also those who would like to see different changes to the FISA Court than the ones I've proposed. On all these issues, I am open to working with Congress to ensure that we build a broad consensus for how to move forward, and I'm confident that we can shape an approach that meets our security needs while upholding the civil liberties of every American. . . .

For ultimately, what's at stake in this debate goes far beyond a few months of headlines, or passing tensions in our foreign policy. When you cut through the noise, what's really at stake is how we remain true to who we are in a world that is remaking itself at dizzying speed. Whether it's the ability of individuals to communicate ideas; to access information that would have once filled every great library in every country in the world; or to forge bonds with people on other sides of the globe, technology is remaking what is possible for individuals, and for institutions, and for the international order. So while the reforms that I have announced will point us in a new direction, I am mindful that more work will be needed in the future.

One thing I'm certain of. This debate will make us stronger. And I also know that in this time of change, the United States of America will have to lead. . . .

As the nation that developed the Internet, the world expects us to ensure that the digital revolution works as a tool for individual empowerment, not government control. Having faced down the dangers of totalitarianism and fascism and communism, the world expects us to stand up for the principle that every person has the right to think and write and form relationships freely—because individual freedom is the wellspring of human progress.

5

Can Congress Oversee the NSA?

Zoë Carpenter

Zoë Carpenter is a reporter in the Nation's *Washington, DC, bureau. She has written for* Rolling Stone, Guernica, *and the* Poughkeepsie Journal, *among other publications.*

The mechanisms for oversight that have long been in place to keep tabs on the activities of America's intelligence-gathering and surveillance programs have become out of date, and those charged with the responsibility are no longer effective as watchdogs. Congressional committees now have limited power in the face of gigantic, secretive security agencies. They are often given inaccurate testimony and insufficient briefings about activities and have little way to discover the inconsistencies or to challenge them. Committee members themselves are often more inclined to support security agencies than to scrutinize them. Congress should make a variety of changes to strengthen the integrity and authority of oversight bodies so that the public can trust that the activities of security agencies are being properly monitored.

"The men and women of America's intelligence agencies are overwhelmingly dedicated professionals," Ron Wyden said on Wednesday, before proceeding to excoriate their bosses in front of the Senate Intelligence Committee. Addressing Director of Intelligence James Clapper, CIA Director John Brennan and FBI Director James Comey, Wyden continued,

Zoë Carpenter, "Can Congress Oversee the NSA?," *The Nation* (blog), January 30, 2014. www.thenation.com/blog. Reproduced by permission.

"They deserve to have leadership that is trusted by the American people. Unfortunately, that trust has been seriously undermined by senior officials' reckless reliance on secret interpretations of the law and battered by years of misleading and deceptive statements that senior officials made to the American people. These statements did not protect sources and methods that were useful in fighting terror. Instead, they hid bad policy choices and violation of the liberties of the American people."

With the future of the surveillance programs disclosed by Edward Snowden still uncertain, the ball is very much in Congress's court. Specifically, in the Intelligence and Judiciary Committees, which have critical oversight roles over the National Security Agency and others. The stakes are higher than the individual programs revealed by Snowden, however. In question is Congress's ability to act as an effective watchdog over an expanding national security state.

In essence, the delicate balance Congress sought to strike thirty-five years ago now appears to be tipped, rather decisively, in favor of the intelligence community.

Wednesday's hearing nicely showcased the two major hurdles to congressional oversight. The first, as Wyden argued, is senior intelligence officials. The second is the congressional committees, which face an institutional mismatch with the intelligence community and whose members often seem more committed to protecting, rather than scrutinizing, the agencies they are tasked with overseeing.

First, a brief history. After revelations about abuses by the CIA and other agencies in the 1970s, Congress struck what Stephen Vladeck, a professor of law at American University, calls a "grand bargain," to accommodate the paradoxical need to submit secret programs to democratic oversight. New legal constraints on intelligence activities would be enforced not in public but instead behind the veil by the intelligence committees and the Foreign Intelligence Surveillance Court (also known as the FISA court). As Colorado Senator Mark Udall said at the Intelligence Committee hearing, "This committee was created to address a severe breach of trust that developed when it was revealed that the CIA was conducting unlawful domestic searches."

The Snowden leaks indicate the bargain has broken down. "In essence, the delicate balance Congress sought to strike thirty-five years ago now appears to be tipped, rather decisively, in favor of the intelligence community," Vladeck explained in an e-mail.

Intelligence officials have done some of that tipping themselves, by withholding information from the public and lawmakers. On Wednesday, Wyden said the committee had been "stonewalled" by intelligence officials; indeed, none of his questions received direct answers, although Wyden did receive promises from officials to get back to him by specific deadlines.

Wyden also cited several incidents in which officials had given inaccurate testimony in public hearings. Last March, for example, James Clapper told Wyden that the NSA did "not wittingly" collect data on American citizens, a claim we now know from the Snowden leaks to be false.

In some cases, officials may not be telling legislators anything at all. "There are certain things that the committees are simply not going to find out about unless they're briefed," said Representative Adam Schiff, a California Democrat on the House Intelligence Committee. According to law, the executive branch must keep the intelligence committees "fully and currently informed" of any intelligence activity, including significant anticipated activity. But recent history suggests that even committee chairs have not been kept abreast. Senator Dianne Feinstein, who chairs the Senate Intelligence Committee and has become one of the NSA's closest congressional allies, has admitted that her committee "was not satisfactorily informed" about certain surveillance activities, in particular the tapping of German chancellor Angela Merkel's cell phone.

Whether Congress has the will to strengthen its own hand is the big question.

The reauthorization of Section 215 of the Patriot Act, which the NSA says provides legal grounds for collecting Americans' phone records in bulk, presents another case in which Congress appears to have had insufficient information to determine whether intelligence activities were lawful. In a report released last Friday, the Privacy and Civil Liberties Oversight Board explained that the FISC did not articulate the legal basis for bulk collection until last August—years after Congress extended Section 215 in 2010 and 2011. This indicates that lawmakers may not have been properly informed of how the statute was being applied when they extended it. Ultimately, the board argued that Section 215 is not written in a way that justifies bulk data collection at all, but it said that even if the language were ambiguous, some members of Congress "may have been prohibited from reading" critical documents before voting to maintain Section 215.

One explanation for these gaps is the institutional mismatch between the intelligence community and the congressional committees. "The intelligence committees are small, the staff is small, the agencies themselves are behemoth," said Schiff. In the House, members are not permitted to have their own staff on the committee, and some have described feeling inadequately prepared to question intelligence officials. "You don't have any idea what kind of things are going on. So you have to start just spitting off random questions: Does the government have a moon base? Does the government have a talking bear? Does the government have a cyborg army?" Representative Justin Amash said in October at a conference hosted by the Cato Institute.

The administration says Congress is duly informed, while other lawmakers have suggested it's their colleagues' own fault if they aren't up to speed. Clapper reaffirmed promises of greater transparency on Wednesday, but critics remain skeptical. "I don't think this culture of misinformation is going to be easily fixed," Wyden warned. Representative Schiff told me that he expects the mismatch in resources to continue to impact the committees' oversight ability. "I'd like to see our capacities augmented in the intelligence committee, but at a time of dwindling legislative budgets, I'm not sure whether that will take place," he said.

Congress could reassert some of its own authority by including more members in the group briefed on significant intelligence activity, for example; by shortening the authorization period for laws like the Patriot Act to spur more frequent debate; by imposing a rule of lenity on the FISA court, so that the administration would have to receive congressional approval in ambiguous cases, thus preventing the FISA court from creating its own novel interpretations of law; and by making sure FISA judges hear adversarial opinions from civil liberties and technology experts. Whether Congress has the will to strengthen its own hand is the big question. The fact that the chairman of the House Intelligence Committee, Mike Rogers, believes that "you can't have your privacy violated if you don't know your privacy is violated" does not exactly inspire confidence.

These questions about oversight can and should be separated from the debate about the legality and effectiveness of individual surveillance programs. "It may well be, at the end of the day, that the programs the committees are overseeing are legal, but meaningful oversight presupposes that the overseers will be the last, not the first, to reach that conclusion," said Vladeck. The decision about whether the government or anyone else may continue to sweep up and search our phone records is important. Without addressing broader oversight issues, however, we may barely scratch the surface of a much-needed conversation about balance of power in the post-9/11 era.

6

Strong Oversight of Intelligence Gathering Protects Civil Rights

Alexander W. Joel

Alexander W. Joel is the civil liberties protection officer for the Office of the Director of National Intelligence.

The job of a civil liberties protection officer is to work with the government's various intelligence and security agencies to ensure Americans' civil liberties and privacy rights are protected. That officer works with a large team of professionals to make sure that US intelligence-gathering and surveillance activities are constitutional and do not violate any laws. There are several layers of oversight for various activities, ranging from laws and agency regulations to oversight boards, congressional committees, and special courts, such as the Foreign Intelligence Surveillance Act (FISA) Court. These bodies are all charged with ensuring the legality of security programs, and protecting civil liberties and privacy is a responsibility that everyone who works in the intelligence community takes very seriously.

Many Americans probably don't know that there is a senior official whose job by law is to help ensure that civil liberties and privacy protections are built into intelligence programs. I am that official—the "Civil Liberties Protection Officer." I engage with the director of national intelligence and other intelligence officials to oversee and guide intelligence activities.

Alexander W. Joel, "The Job of Protecting Security and Privacy," *McClatchy-Tribune*, August 13, 2013. Reproduced by permission.

I lead a team of experts who coordinate not only with intelligence operators and analysts, but also with government lawyers, inspectors general, compliance officials and oversight boards, to help shape intelligence activities and oversee their implementation. As the intelligence agencies seek to protect the nation's security, they must also protect civil liberties and privacy.

Explaining to the public how all of this comes together is important, but is hard to do because it involves sensitive information that adversaries could exploit to avoid detection. By definition, most intelligence work can't be done openly. A fully transparent intelligence service, after all, could not be an effective one.

Under the Section 702 program, the government can only obtain foreign intelligence information as defined by law. . . . This authority cannot be used to intentionally target United States persons or anyone inside the United States.

Mistrust Is Natural

It's human nature for such secrecy to fuel suspicion and mistrust. People assume that when someone hides something, it's because he's doing something wrong. This natural suspicion is evident in the concerns about two programs that were recently disclosed: the telephone metadata program conducted under the "business records" provision of the Foreign Intelligence Surveillance Act [FISA] (which was amended by Section 215 of the PATRIOT Act [The USA PATRIOT Act, officially titled the Uniting and Strengthening America by Providing Appropriate Tools Required to Intercept and Obstruct Terrorism Act of 2001]), and the collection of communications from foreign intelligence targets who are non-U.S. persons located outside the United States, conducted under Section 702 of

FISA. The Office of the Director of National Intelligence [ODNI] has published a significant amount of information about both of these programs on its public website, www .dni.gov.

Because these are complicated programs, I want to address a few publicly discussed concerns here in a non-legalistic way.

Under the phone metadata program, the government obtains and reviews phone records only to identify whether telephones associated with a foreign terrorist organization are in communication with a telephone inside the United States (directly or indirectly). This does not involve collecting actual phone conversations. While the government believes that it has been carrying out this program in a manner that protects both national security and privacy, we are carefully exploring alternatives with the congressional oversight committees to address public concerns.

Under the Section 702 program, the government can only obtain foreign intelligence information as defined by law, using court-approved procedures to identify specific foreign intelligence targets outside the United States. This authority cannot be used to intentionally target United States persons or anyone inside the United States.

Several Layers of Scrutiny

If the government is focusing on a foreign intelligence target abroad, and incidentally obtains a communication between that target and a United States person (or discussing a United States person), what happens? Section 702 requires that such communications be carefully handled only as specifically authorized by court-approved procedures; for example, information identifying a U.S. person may only be included in an intelligence report if it is necessary to understand the foreign intelligence being reported.

Compliance under these programs is verified by several layers of oversight. For example, my office jointly oversees the

Section 702 program with the Department of Justice. We verify that potential compliance incidents are documented and reported, and that any improperly collected information is purged from government systems. We regularly visit the facilities involved, review audit records, talk directly to the analysts, and submit our findings to Congress and the FISA Court.

Mistakes happen, and when they do, they are taken seriously. To date, we have found errors caused by inadvertence or technical problems, but have not found an intentional violation (which could result in criminal penalties, with fines of up to $10,000 and imprisonment of up to five years).

Oversight Boards

Oversight boards are also involved. The President's Intelligence Oversight Board reviews reports of potential violations. The Privacy and Civil Liberties Oversight Board, an independent federal agency, is currently conducting an in-depth review of these two programs, and has full access to classified information about them and to the personnel involved. My office works with both boards to ensure that they are receiving the information they need to perform their oversight functions.

In my experience, intelligence professionals—and those overseeing them—are profoundly committed to the oath they take to support and defend the Constitution.

Congress also provides oversight, through the intelligence oversight committees, which were established specifically to provide a venue in which classified intelligence activities could be comprehensively discussed and reviewed. Both programs are regularly briefed to the congressional oversight committees.

And in the FISA Court, the government's activities are strictly supervised. The Court is composed of regular federal district court judges, who take their responsibilities seriously, and act with care and deliberation. These judges are by no means a "rubber stamp." During my office's regular engagements with government officials on matters before the Court, I have been impressed with how rigorously the Court oversees government activities.

Can the Government Be Trusted?

Some people question whether people who work for the government can be trusted. In my experience, intelligence professionals—and those overseeing them—are profoundly committed to the oath they take to support and defend the Constitution. People inside government have questions and concerns just like everyone else. It's my job to raise civil liberties and privacy issues about intelligence activities, and I do. If intelligence personnel have legal or civil liberties concerns, they can raise them in secure ways, including by contacting my office, offices of inspector general, or the congressional oversight committees. Under law, they are protected from reprisal if they do.

Can more public transparency be provided? We recognize how crucial this is to earning and retaining public trust, and are working to provide it in a way that does not compromise the nation's security. In addition to posting information about both these programs on its public website, the ODNI just declassified additional documents pertaining to the phone metadata program.

Protecting civil liberties and privacy in the conduct of our intelligence activities is not my job alone; it is the job of every intelligence professional. No one is perfect, of course, and it is important to examine carefully different alternatives that enable the intelligence community to fulfill its core mission of serving the American people, under the law, in a manner that protects both their security and their freedom. While there are undoubtedly ways to do this job differently, I hope no one doubts our commitment to get it right.

7

Americans Can't Find Out Whether the Government Watches Them

Marisa Taylor and Jonathan Landay

Marisa Taylor is an investigative reporter and Jonathan Landay is a national security and intelligence reporter for McClatchy Newspapers, based in Washington, DC.

The National Security Agency (NSA) is turning down requests from individuals who want to find out whether the agency is holding records of their telephone communications. Simply answering yes or no, the NSA argues, is classified information that would jeopardize the effectiveness of its data-collection program. That means that innocent people whose communications data may be held by the agency have no way of even finding out. The NSA's refusal to provide that information is based on a legal precedent called a "Glomar denial," which claims that simply acknowledging the existence or nonexistence of a document would give away vital national secrets. Transparency advocates say instead that it allows the NSA to hide the agency's unchecked civil rights abuses.

Since last year's [2013] revelations about the National Security Agency's [NSA] massive communications data dragnets, the spy agency has been inundated with requests from Americans and others wanting to know if it has files on them. All of them are being turned down.

Marisa Taylor and Jonathan Landay, "Americans Find Swift Stonewall on Whether NSA Vacuumed Their Data," *McClatchy DC* online, February 11, 2014. www.mcclatchydc .com. Reproduced by permission.

The denials illustrate the bind in which the disclosures have trapped the [Barack] Obama administration. While it has pledged to provide greater transparency about the NSA's communications collections, the NSA says it cannot respond to individuals' requests without tipping off terrorists and other targets.

As a result, Americans whose email and telephone data may have been improperly vacuumed up have no way of finding that out by filing open records requests with the agency. Six McClatchy reporters who filed requests seeking any information kept by the NSA on them all received the same response.

"Were we to provide positive or negative responses to requests such as yours, our adversaries' compilation of the information provided would reasonably be expected to cause exceptionally grave damage to the national security," the NSA wrote last month [January 2014] in response to a McClatchy national security reporter who requested his own records. "Therefore, your request is denied because the fact of the existence or non-existence of responsive records is a currently and properly classified matter."

In what is known as a Glomar denial, the NSA and other federal agencies can respond to records requests that by acknowledging the existence of relevant documents, vital secrets would be disclosed.

In an apparent reaction to former NSA contractor Edward Snowden's revelations of the NSA's data collections, the number of open records requests filed with the agency more than tripled—from 1,065 to 4,060—between 2010 and 2013, according to data supplied by the NSA. The denial rate during the same period skyrocketed from an estimated 33 percent to 82 percent because of the higher number of people seeking their own intelligence records. The NSA does approve other types of records requests, such as academics asking for historic records and former workers seeking their employment records.

Glomar Denials

The high rejection rate of requests seeking individuals' own records sharply contrasts with Director of National Intelligence James R. Clapper's pledge to "lean in the direction of transparency, wherever and whenever we can." It also clashes with the NSA's own public assertion that laws enacted in 1974 entitle "individuals to access federal agency records or to request an amendment to records that are maintained in a file retrievable by an individual's name."

In what is known as a Glomar denial, the NSA and other federal agencies can respond to records requests that by acknowledging the existence of relevant documents, vital secrets would be disclosed. The term stems from a salvage ship, the Glomar Explorer, which was built with the secret mission of recovering a Soviet nuclear submarine that sank in the Pacific Ocean in 1968.

A subsequent Freedom of Information court suit seeking CIA [Central Intelligence Agency] records on the operation established the loophole when a court upheld the CIA's refusal to confirm or deny the existence of those files on national security grounds.

"Theoretically, these agencies could argue that al Qaida could get everyone on Earth to file a request (for documents) and by process of elimination find out who they're really spying on," said Kel McClanahan, an attorney who specializes in suing intelligence agencies under open records laws. "It may be a ludicrous argument, but it's one that the agencies are able to assert."

Operating in Secrecy

NSA spokeswoman Vanee Vines said that although her agency must deny individuals' requests for their own intelligence files, her agency releases as much information as it deems possible in other cases.

"The administration's push for transparency is taken very seriously by the FOIA (Freedom of Information Act) Office at NSA," she said. "Because it is not possible to use discretion to release classified information, the FOIA Office does its best to release other information that could potentially be protected under another exemption if a specific harm to the agency is not identified."

Vines also said the numbers cited by McClatchy might be misleading because they do not reveal the number of pages of documents or the significance of the information released. The number of cases where the NSA released all of the documents requested has increased from 49 in 2010 to 82 in 2013, she pointed out.

Documents released by the administration in response to Snowden's leaks have confirmed that the NSA violated its own rules in some cases, including by improperly collecting at least 56,000 domestic emails.

"Looking at the growing numbers of partial denials or full denials does not mean that NSA is releasing less information," Vines said.

Some transparency advocates, however, said the NSA's ability to sidestep individuals' requests allows the agency to hide its own abuses.

"This is part of the reason why intelligence agencies are spiraling out of control," said Mark Rumold, an attorney with the Electronic Frontier Foundation, a nonprofit group that has pressed the administration to release documents related to surveillance. "These agencies have an ability to operate in utter secrecy."

Agency Violated Its Own Rules

Documents released by the administration in response to Snowden's leaks have confirmed that the NSA violated its own rules in some cases, including by improperly collecting at least 56,000 domestic emails as part of its massive surveillance program to combat terrorism. A federal court ruled the program unconstitutional, forcing the NSA to change its practices by segregating collections most likely to contain Americans' emails.

The NSA has not publicly revealed details about those cases, however.

Other agencies have kept such collection under wraps as well.

The Drug Enforcement Administration [DEA] trained its agents how to conceal evidence used in criminal investigations but gathered from various sources, including from NSA intercepts, the Reuters news agency found last year [2013]. As a result, the DEA did not notify defendants and even some prosecutors and judges how it had obtained the evidence.

Separately, the Justice Department had concluded that some criminal defendants did not need to be told about NSA surveillance unless email or telephone records gathered during the intercepts were filed as evidence in a criminal case, according to a *New York Times* report. The policy applied to surveillance authorized under the 2008 law that permitted warrantless eavesdropping on overseas communications.

After media reports drew attention to the loophole, the Justice Department late last year for the first time notified a criminal defendant that evidence against him would include NSA intercepts. The defendant, Jamshid Muhtorov, was accused in 2012 of providing material support to an Uzbek terrorist group. The American Civil Liberties Union is now seeking to have the evidence thrown out as part of its challenge to the constitutionality of the NSA's programs.

Journalists Were Monitored

During the George W. Bush administration, the Justice Department's inspector general uncovered widespread abuses in FBI programs that relied on administrative or emergency orders to obtain telephone records. As a result of the scrutiny, the FBI disclosed in 2008 that it had improperly collected the phone records of *Washington Post* and *New York Times* reporters four years earlier. It's unknown whether other journalists have been monitored improperly.

Last month, the FBI refused to rule out whether it had information about several McClatchy journalists, although it's likely that the FBI had records at some point related to one of the reporters. In 2007, the FBI opened a leak investigation to determine the sources for the reporter's stories on a public corruption investigation.

"We were unable to identify main file records," the bureau said in its responses to that reporter and others, adding that it could neither confirm nor deny that any of the journalists were on watch lists.

To prevent future surveillance abuses, Congress might need to allow certain categories of American citizens to request their records, such as in cases where there is evidence of misconduct by an agency, some experts said.

"You can't do effective oversight of NSA surveillance on a retail basis by submitting lots and lots of individual Freedom of Information Act requests," said Steven Aftergood, head of the Federation of the American Scientists' Project on Government Secrecy. "This is a policy issue that needs to be debated and resolved in Congress."

8

Domestic Surveillance Has a Chilling Effect on Political Speech

John W. Whitehead

John W. Whitehead is an attorney and president of the Rutherford Institute, a nonprofit civil liberties and human rights organization.

The fact that the government can now, at any time, access entire phone conversations, e-mail exchanges, and other communications from months or years past should frighten every American. But it mostly doesn't because the public has come to accept such intrusion into their lives as a byproduct of ensuring public safety in a climate of fear, following such events as September 11, 2001, or the Boston Marathon bombing in 2013. The reality that all digital communications are now monitored is dangerous for free speech, as evidenced by the Massachusetts teen who was jailed on terrorism charges over rap lyrics he posted on Facebook. The government has become a bigger threat to American freedoms than the terrorist groups these security agencies were designed to thwart.

> "If you're not a terrorist, if you're not a threat, prove it. This is the price you pay to live in free society right now. It's just the way it is."
>
> *Sergeant Ed Mullins of the New York Police Department*

John W. Whitehead, "Round the Clock Surveillance: Is This the Price of Living in a 'Free, Safe' Society?," The Rutherford Institute, May 13, 2013. www.rutherford.org. Reproduced by permission.

Immediately following the devastating 9/11 [2001] attacks, which destroyed the illusion of invulnerability which had defined American society since the end of the Cold War, many Americans willingly ceded their rights and liberties to government officials who promised them that the feeling of absolute safety could be restored.

In the [13] years since, we have been subjected to a series of deceptions, subterfuges and scare tactics by the government, all largely aimed at amassing more power for the federal agencies and extending their control over the populace. Starting with the wars in Afghanistan and Iraq, continuing with the torture of detainees at Abu Ghraib and Guantanamo Bay [military prisons], and coming to a head with the assassination of American citizens abroad, the importing of drones and other weapons of compliance, and the rise in domestic surveillance, we have witnessed the onslaught of a full-blown crisis in government.

Now, in the wake of the Boston Marathon bombing, we are once again being assured that if we only give up a few more liberties and what little remains of our privacy, we will achieve that elusive sense of security we've yet to attain.

Still Americans have gone along with these assaults on their freedoms unquestioningly.

Even with our freedoms in shambles, our country in debt, our so-called "justice" system weighted in favor of corporations and the police state, our government officials dancing to the tune of corporate oligarchs, and a growing intolerance on the part of the government for anyone who challenges the status quo, Americans have yet to say "enough is enough."

Now, in the wake of the Boston Marathon bombing [April 2013], we are once again being assured that if we only give up a few more liberties and what little remains of our privacy, we will achieve that elusive sense of security we've yet to attain. This is the same song and dance that comes after every tragedy, and it's that same song and dance which has left us buying into the illusion that we are a free, safe society.

All Digital Communications Are Monitored

The reality of life in America tells a different tale, however. For example, in a May 2013 interview with CNN, former FBI [Federal Bureau of Investigation] counterterrorism agent Tim Clemente disclosed that the federal government is keeping track of *all* digital communications that occur within the United States, whether or not those communicating are American citizens, and whether or not they have a warrant to do so.

As revelatory as the disclosure was, it caused barely a ripple of dismay among Americans, easily distracted by the torrent of what passes for entertainment news today. Yet it confirms what has become increasingly apparent in the years after 9/11: the federal government is literally tracking any and all communications occurring within the United States, without concern for the legal limitations of such activity, and without informing the American people that they are doing so.

Clemente dropped his bombshell during a CNN interview about authorities' attempts to determine the nature of communications between deceased Boston bombing suspect Tamerlan Tsarnaev and his widow Katherine Russell. In the course of that conversation, Clemente revealed that federal officials will not only be able to access any voicemails that may have been left by either party, but that the entirety of the phone conversations they had will be at federal agents' finger tips.

"We certainly have ways in national security investigations to find out exactly what was said in that conversation," stated Clemente. "All of that stuff [meaning phone conversations occurring in America] is being captured as we speak whether we know it or like it or not." A few days later, Clemente was asked to clarify his comments, at which point he said, "There is a way to look at all digital communications in the past. No digital communication is secure."

Officials in the Obama administration have for some time now been authorizing corporate information sharing and spying in secret through the use of executive orders and other tactics.

In other words, there is no form of digital communication that the government cannot and does not monitor—phone calls, emails, text messages, tweets, Facebook posts, internet video chats, etc., are all *accessible, trackable and downloadable* by federal agents.

Privacy Online Is Now Only an Illusion

At one time, such actions by the government would not only have been viewed as unacceptable, they would also have been considered illegal. However, government officials have been engaged in an ongoing attempt to legitimize these actions by passing laws that make the lives of all Americans an open book for government agents. For example, while the nation was caught up in the drama of the Boston bombing and the ensuing military-style occupation of the city by local and federal police, Congress passed a little-noticed piece of legislation known as the Cyber Intelligence Sharing and Protection Act (CISPA). The legislation, which the House of Representatives approved by an overwhelming margin of 288–127, will allow internet companies to share their users' private data with the federal government and other private companies in order to combat so-called "cyber threats."

In short, the law dismantles any notion of privacy on the internet, opening every action one undertakes online, whether emailing, shopping, banking, or just browsing, to scrutiny by government agents. While CISPA has yet to clear the U.S. Senate Committee on Commerce, Science, and Transportation, the spirit of it is alive and well. In fact, officials in the [Barack] Obama administration have for some time now been authorizing corporate information sharing and spying in secret through the use of executive orders and other tactics.

The Justice Department, for instance, has been issuing so-called "2511 letters" to various internet service providers like AT&T, which immunize them from being prosecuted under federal wiretapping laws for providing the federal government with private information. Despite federal court rulings to the contrary, the Department of Justice continues to assert that it does not require a warrant to access Americans' emails, Facebook chats, and other forms of digital communication.

How It All Started

While it may be tempting to lay the full blame for these erosions of our privacy on the Obama administration, they are simply continuing a system of mass surveillance, the seeds of which were planted in the weeks after 9/11, when the National Security Agency (NSA) began illegally tracking the communications of American citizens. According to a *Washington Post* article published in 2010, the NSA continues to collect 1.7 billion communications, whether telephone, email or otherwise, *every single day.*

> *Aside from allowing government agents backdoor access to American communications, corporations are also working on technologies to allow government agents even easier access to Americans' communications.*

The NSA and Department of Justice are just two pieces of a vast surveillance network which encompasses and implicates most of the federal government, as well as the majority of technology and telecommunications companies in the United States. For the past two years, the United States Foreign Intelligence Surveillance Court has approved literally every single request by the federal government to spy on people within the United States. There have been some 4,000 applications rubberstamped by the court in the past two years, applications which allow federal officials to monitor the communications of any person in the United States, including American citizens, if they are believed to be in contact with someone overseas.

These government-initiated spying programs depend in large part on the willingness of corporations to hand over personal information about their customers to government officials. Sometimes the government purchases the information outright. At other times, the government issues National Security Letters, which allow the government to force companies to hand over personal information without a warrant or probable cause.

Tech Companies Get Onboard

Some web companies, such as Skype, have already altered their products to allow government access to personal information. In fact, government agents can now determine the credit card information and addresses of Skype users under suspicion of criminal activity. Aside from allowing government agents backdoor access to American communications, corporations are also working on technologies to allow government agents even easier access to Americans' communications.

For example, Google has filed a patent for a "Policy Violation Checker," software which would monitor an individual's communications as they type them out, whether in an email, an Excel spreadsheet or some other digital document, then alert the individual, and potentially their employer or a government agent, if they type any "problematic phrases" which "present policy violations, have legal implications, or are otherwise troublesome to a company, business, or individual."

The software would work by comparing the text being typed to a pre-defined database of "problematic phrases," which would presumably be defined on a company-by-company basis.

The emergence of this technology fits in well with Google chairman Eric Schmidt's view on privacy, which is that "If you have something that you don't want anyone to know, maybe you shouldn't be doing it in the first place." Unfortunately, this is not just the attitude of corporate benefactors who stand to profit from creating spy technology and software but government officials as well.

Monitoring Social Media in Real Time

Additionally, police officials throughout the country have become increasingly keen on monitoring social media websites in real time. Rob D'Ovido, a criminal justice professor at Drexel University, has noted that, "The danger of this in light of the tragedy in Boston is that law enforcement is being so risk-averse they are in danger of crossing that line and going after what courts would ultimately deem as free speech."

Having traded our freedoms for a phantom promise of security, we now find ourselves imprisoned in a virtual cage of cameras, wiretaps and watchful government eyes.

For example, Cameron Dambrosio, a teenager and self-styled rap artist living in Metheun, Massachusetts, posted a video of one of his original songs on the internet which included references to the White House and the Boston bombing. While the song's lyrics may well have been crude and ill-advised in the wake of the Boston bombing, police officers exacerbated the situation by arresting Dambrosio [in May 2013] and charging him with communicating terrorist threats, a felony charge which could land him in prison for twenty years.

Unfortunately, cases like Dambrosio's may soon become the norm, as the FBI's Next Generation Cyber Initiative has announced that its "top legislative priority" this year is to get social media giants like Facebook and Google to comply with requests for access to real-time updates of social media websites. The proposed method of encouraging compliance is legal inquiries and hefty fines leveled at these companies. The Obama administration is expected to support the proposal.

The reality is this: we no longer live in a free society. Having traded our freedoms for a phantom promise of security, we now find ourselves imprisoned in a virtual cage of cameras, wiretaps and watchful government eyes. All the while, the world around us is no safer than when we started on this journey more than a decade ago. Indeed, it well may be that we are living in a far more dangerous world, not so much because the terrorist threat is any greater but because the government itself has become the greater threat to our freedoms.

9

Surveillance Should Be Embraced to Create a Transparent Society

David Brin

David Brin is a scientist and science-fiction author whose seminal nonfiction book, The Transparent Society: Will Technology Force Us to Choose Between Privacy and Freedom? *won the American Library Association's Freedom of Speech award.*

There is no way to turn back the clock on technology—it is here to stay, and citizens and authorities both face the same choice: fight the developments or embrace them. The best thing for society is to adapt to the evolving technologies and accept the ubiquity of surveillance cameras so that society can evolve and become truly transparent. Watching the watchers is the best way to keep them honest, and the best way to accomplish this is with "sousveillance," the widespread recording of events by their participants. Sousveillance is the only way to stop surveillance data from being controlled by the powerful. It levels the playing field so that true transparency and true accountability are assured from all players.

It seems that almost daily, some elite is outed for snooping. The National Security Agency [NSA] monitored traffic patterns from U.S. telephones. The Prism program accessed troves of customer data from Internet firms like Microsoft and Apple. British intelligence used public websites to spy on diplomats.

David Brin, "Lessons for an Age of Transparency," *New Perspectives Quarterly* online, July 22, 2013. www.digitalnpq.org. Reproduced by permission.

The U.S. Postal Service has been logging our physical mail. The FBI [Federal Bureau of Investigation] admits using drones to tail suspects within the U.S. News media are outraged by governmental leak investigations, while celebrities and politicians denounce spy outrages by news organizations. Corporations swap our information for profit, without consultation or constraint.

Meanwhile, alarmed pundits denounce a new tool, Google Glass, that lets uber-geeks record everything they see while overlaying meta-data upon the Real World.

Much of today's hand-wringing focuses rightfully on potential abuse of power. Both ends of the hoary political spectrum disagree over whether to most fear government or a rising corporate oligarchy, but all paladins of liberty share one dread: that despots will be tech-empowered by universal surveillance.

An Explosion of Technology

And what did you expect? Ever since the discovery of printing and glass lenses, each generation (in the West) acquired new prosthetics to expand human vision, memory and reach. Waves of innovation—from print journalism and libraries to radio, television and the Internet—promised liberation or oppression. Citizens and societies were disrupted, cajoled, misled . . . and adapted.

The more open society becomes, the smaller, more temporary and closely held your secrets had better be.

So, is there a bigger perspective to this latest phase? Look again at [WikiLeak's] Julian Assange, [Army jailed private] Bradley Manning, [former NSA contractor] Edward Snowden or the Swiss bank employees who recently exposed their secretive masters to cleansing light. More significant than any specific revelation is what these knights-errant and countless others represent about our time. Spanning the range from brave whistleblowers revealing the illegal and heinous, all the way to preening indignation junkies (often blending both extremes), they are just what you'd expect from a society whose pop media endlessly preach eccentric individualism and suspicion of authority.

Which brings us to Lesson No. 1: *Oh ye mighty, whether you qualify as conspirators or protectors, you must limit the number of your henchmen.*

No array of security clearances and lie detectors will prevent these hemorrhages. Not when your agency employs half a million "trusted" employees and contractors. Nor will it seal the dikes to make an example of some self-styled hero. The more open society becomes, the smaller, more temporary and closely held your secrets had better be.

Unintended Consequences

Want to see the future of unintended consequences? With stunning agility, attorneys in divorce, murder and other cases have filed demands to access the NSA's freshly revealed database of U.S. telephone call traffic links, as a vital resource to exculpate their clients. Now picture the world not one year from now, but a decade from now.

Lesson No. 2: *Authorities, you can either fight this new era or embrace it.*

Those who resist the trend will follow the obstinate reflexes of history and human nature. But the future will be won by agile ones applying judo, not sumo. Sure, earnest officials in our professional protector caste still need tactical secrecy, short-term and targeted, for many tasks. But only fools ignore the benefits of a secular trend toward an open world. Consider: Among the foes who would do us grievous harm—from terrorists to hostile states to criminal gangs—can you name one that's not fatally allergic to light? In contrast, modern democracies find light occasionally irksome, generally bracing and mostly healthy. That difference is the paramount strategic consideration of the 21st century.

Put it another way: No combination of FBI or CIA [Central Intelligence Agency] intelligence coups could possibly hamper the schemes of external foes more thoroughly than for those rival powers to suffer wave after wave of their own Edward Snowdens.

Lesson No. 3: *Bad things like 9/11 will happen.*

Not a Zero-Sum Game

When they do, members of our protector caste will claim they might have thwarted calamity if provided greater powers to see, know, analyze, anticipate and reach. Amid panic and public alarm, those powers will be granted. Top-down surveillance will augment in a forward ratchet that's hard to rewind. Sure, a decade after 9/11 we may now curb (a little) some warrantless surveillance by NSA and FBI. But such efforts miss the point, because they buy into the notion of a dichotomy—a zero-sum tradeoff—between security and freedom.

The answer isn't to cower or hide from Big Brother, nor to blind our watchdogs. The solution is to answer surveillance with sousveillance.

It is fallacious to base our freedom and safety upon blinding elites. First, can you name one time in human annals when that actually happened? When those on top forsook any powers of vision? Forbid, and you'll drive it underground, as happened when the "Total Information Awareness" program scurried away from public attention, finding darker corners in which to grow. As author Robert Heinlein said, the chief effect of a privacy law is to "make the (spy) bugs smaller."

And smaller they become! Faster than Moore's law [that overall processing power for computers will double every two years], cameras get cheaper, better, more mobile, more numerous and smaller each year. Your Google Glass "specs" may provoke strong objections today, while they resemble Borg [fictional alien race] implants. Tomorrow they'll look like normal sunglasses. A few years later, they will vanish into contact lenses. (Prototypes exist.) If laws banish such things, who will be thwarted? Only normal folk, while elites—government, corporate, wealth, criminal and foreign—will have the new omniscience. How do you propose stopping them? Indeed, should we? Recall how the Boston Marathon bombers were rapidly caught thanks to a ubiquity of cameras, nearly all of them privately owned.

Hence, Lesson No. 4 is much like Lesson No. 2: *Citizens, you can either fight this new era or embrace it.*

What Is "Sousveillance"?

"I do not want to live in a world where everything I do and say is recorded," proclaimed Snowden, with unintended irony, as he ripped veils off those he disliked. But as I held in *The Transparent Society*, the answer isn't to cower or hide from Big Brother, nor to blind our watchdogs. The solution is to answer surveillance with sousveillance [the recording of events by their participants], or looking back at the mighty from below. Holding light accountable with reciprocal light. Letting our watchdogs see but imposing choke-chain limits on what they do. That distinction is crucial. Instead of obsessing on what the FBI and NSA may know, let's demand fierce tools of supervision to keep the dog from becoming a wolf.

Start by replacing the secret, star-chamber FISA [Foreign Intelligence Surveillance Act] court with one that is confidential but adversarially contested and accountable, as any true court should be. Put a short time limit on the gag orders in national security letters, making them less terrifyingly Orwellian [referring to writings of George Orwell, paticularly his novel, *1984*]. Take today's inspectors general out of bed with the agencies they oversee, and have them answer instead to an Inspector General of the United States, whose first duty is to the law, and to us.

Above all, stop obsessing on lines in the sand, fussing over redefining "warrantless searches." Trying to impose limits to what inherently cannot be limited. Change the truly scary parts of the Patriot Act [The USA PATRIOT Act, officially titled the Uniting and Strengthening America by Providing Appropriate Tools Required to Intercept and Obstruct Terrorism Act of 2001], that let authorities peer at us *unsupervised.*

Adapt to Survive

Those who deride sousveillance as "utopian" ignore one fact: It's what already worked. The great enlightenment method of reciprocal accountability and adversarially determined truth—leveling the playing field by pitting elites against each other—is the very thing that underlies science, markets, democracy and all of our success.

Moreover, it is compatible with major trends. Take recent court rulings—and [Barack] Obama administration declarations—that citizens may rightfully record their interactions with police. Perhaps the most vital civil-liberties victory of our time, this shows technology needn't always play the role of villain. And it proves that the forward-ratchet can work in our favor.

What about privacy? Will we trade one Big Brother tyrant for millions of little-brother busybodies? Well, one California company now offers a system that detects lenses a kilometer away, telling soldiers when they're watched. Civilian versions are coming. So, might privacy wind up being defended the way we do it already, in restaurants? By catching snoops in the act?

So here's our final, Big Picture lesson. Suppose we pass this test, adapting to new powers of sight and knowledge the way our ancestors passed every challenge since [Italian physicist] Galileo and [inventor of the printing press Johannes] Gutenberg, somehow surfing a tsunami of change. What one thing will make the crucial difference?

Adapting with resilience, not panic. Finding ways to maximize the good and minimize the bad.

10

NSA Spying Undermines Separation of Powers

Glenn Harlan Reynolds

Glenn Harlan Reynolds is professor of law at the University of Tennessee and the author of The New School: How the Information Age Will Save American Education from Itself.

Most of the bulk data that the National Security Agency (NSA) intercepts from ordinary citizens is of little interest, but the fact is not all citizens are ordinary. Some are political figures, members of Congress, judges, or holders of other sensitive or influential public positions. The federal government's widespread authority to collect data with little oversight undermines the separation of powers and is a threat to constitutional government. Access to such information must be controlled much more tightly to prevent potential abuses for political gain and other personal reasons. There should be strong controls to prevent viewing an individual's records without a warrant, and there should also be an audit trail so the public can see whose information is looked at, by whom, and why.

Most of the worry about the National Security Agency's [NSA] bulk interception of telephone calls, e-mail and the like has centered around threats to privacy. And, in fact, the evidence suggests that if you've got a particularly steamy phone- or Skype-sex session going on, it just might wind up being shared by voyeuristic NSA analysts.

But most Americans figure, probably rightly, that the NSA isn't likely to be interested in their stuff. (Anyone who hacks *my* e-mail is automatically punished, by having to read it.) There is, however, a class of people who can't take that disinterest for granted: members of Congress and the judiciary. What they have to say is likely to be pretty interesting to anyone with a political ax to grind. And the ability of the executive branch to snoop on the phone calls of people in the other branches isn't just a threat to privacy, but a threat to the separation of powers and the Constitution.

As the Framers conceived it, our system of government is divided into three branches—the executive, legislative and judicial—each of which is designed to serve as a check on the others. If the president gets out of control, Congress can defund his efforts, or impeach him, and the judiciary can declare his acts unconstitutional. If Congress passes unconstitutional laws, the president can veto them, or refuse to enforce them, and the judiciary, again, can declare them invalid. If the judiciary gets carried away, the president can appoint new judges, and Congress can change the laws, or even impeach.

Rather than counting on leakers to protect us, we need strong structural controls that don't depend on people being heroically honest or unusually immune to political temptation.

Checks and Balances Out of Whack

But if the federal government has broad domestic-spying powers, and if those are controlled by the executive branch without significant oversight, then the president has the power to snoop on political enemies, getting an advantage in countering their plans, and gathering material that can be used to blackmail or destroy them. With such power in the executive, the traditional role of the other branches as checks would be seriously undermined, and our system of government would veer toward what James Madison in *The Federalist No. 47* called "the very definition of tyranny," that is, "the accumulation of all powers, legislative, executive, and judiciary, in the same hands."

That such widespread spying power exists, of course, doesn't prove that it has actually been abused. But the temptation to make use of such a power for self-serving political ends is likely to be very great. And, given the secrecy surrounding such programs, outsiders might never know. In fact, given the compartmentalization that goes on in the intelligence world, almost everyone at the NSA might be acting properly, completely unaware that one small section is devoted to gather political intelligence. We can hope, of course, that such abuses would leak out, but they might not.

Strong Controls Are Necessary

Rather than counting on leakers to protect us, we need strong structural controls that don't depend on people being heroically honest or unusually immune to political temptation, two characteristics not in oversupply among our political class. That means that the government shouldn't be able to spy on Americans without a warrant—a warrant that comes from a different branch of government, and requires probable cause. The government should also have to keep a clear record of who was spied on, and why, and of exactly who had access to the information once it was gathered. We need the kind of extensive audit trails for access to information that, as the Edward Snowden experience clearly illustrates, don't currently exist.

In addition, we need civil damages—with, perhaps, a waiver of governmental immunities—for abuse of power here. Perhaps we should have bounties for whistleblowers, too, to help encourage wrongdoing to be aired.

Is this strong medicine? Yes. But widespread spying on Americans is a threat to constitutional government. That is a serious disease, one that demands the strongest of medicines.

11

Drones over America: Public Safety Benefit or "Creepy" Privacy Threat?

Anna Mulrine

Anna Mulrine is a staff reporter for the Christian Science Monitor *newspaper.*

With a wide variety of uses ranging from disaster response to traffic reporting, unmanned aerial vehicles (UAVs), or "drones" as they are commonly known, are a hot commodity for cities and law enforcement agencies nationwide. But along with the emergence of the popular new technology has come concern about their capabilities and skepticism about their purported uses. Critics of drones worry that they could be inappropriately used for surveillance of private property or lawful activities such as political protests, or that they could eventually be weaponized. Drone supporters point out that drones so far have very limited capabilities and that there can be no legal expectation of privacy in a public place to begin with. Some American cities have established tough antidrone regulations in anticipation of their growing popularity.

Shortly after Alan Frazier became a part-time deputy sheriff in Grand Forks, N.D., the police began looking into the possibility of buying some aircraft to boost their law enforcement capabilities. They wanted some help doing things like finding missing people or carrying out rescues in a region dotted by farmsteads threatened by flooding that wipes out access to roads.

Buying a turbine engine helicopter, however, would cost $25 million, a prohibitive price tag even with 11 law enforcement agencies—eight from North Dakota and three in western Minnesota—willing to share the cost.

So Mr. Frazier, also an assistant professor of aviation at the University of North Dakota (UND), began looking into unmanned aerial vehicles (UAVs) as a possible alternative.

But what appears, on one level, to be a sensible, practical, and affordable solution for local law enforcement—the price tag for a small UAV is about the cost of a tricked-out new police cruiser at $50,000—has run smack into public concerns about yet another high-tech invasion of privacy and the popular image of drones as stealthy weapons used against terrorists.

The US Border Patrol has the country's largest fleet of UAVs for domestic surveillance, including nine Predator drones that patrol regions like the Rio Grande, searching for illegal immigrants and drug smugglers.

Nonetheless, the technology's potential benefits in pursuing a raft of public safety measures at relatively low cost have enormous appeal for law enforcement agencies across the country, since President Obama signed a bill last year directing the Federal Aviation Administration (FAA) to further open US airspace to drones for both public and private use.

Even before that, the number of permits, known as certificates of authorization (COAs), that the FAA issued to organizations to fly UAVs more than doubled from 146 in 2009 to 313 in 2011. As of February 2013 there were 327 active COAs.

The bulk of these permits go to the US military for training, and the Pentagon expects their numbers to grow considerably in the years to come. According to a March 2011 Pentagon estimate, the Department of Defense will have 197 drones at 105 US bases by 2015.

The US Border Patrol has the country's largest fleet of UAVs for domestic surveillance, including nine Predator drones that patrol regions like the Rio Grande, searching for illegal immigrants and drug smugglers. Unlike the missile-firing Predators used by the Central Intelligence Agency to hunt Al Qaeda operatives and their allies, the domestic version of the aircraft—say, those used by the border patrol—is more typically equipped with night-vision technology and long-range cameras that can read license plates. Groups like the American Civil Liberties Union (ACLU) also complain that these drones have see-through imaging technology similar to those used in airports, as well as facial recognition software tied to federal databases.

The growth in drones is big business. Some 50 companies are developing roughly 150 systems, according to *The Wall Street Journal*, ranging from miniature flying mechanical bugs to "Battlestar Galactica"-type hovering unmanned airplanes. It's an industry expected to reach some $6 billion in US sales by 2016.

Those forecasts notwithstanding, neither the FAA nor the association of UAV operators says it knows how many non-military drones are operating in the United States. The ACLU is seeking that information.

The growth in the development of UAVs by both private companies and the US government has not gone unnoticed, creating a backlash in some communities.

In Seattle last month, community members quashed their city's drone program before it even got started. The program was being considered for search-and-rescue operations and some criminal investigations, but was referred to by protesters as "flying government robots watching their every move."

Mayor Mike McGinn spoke with Police Chief John Diaz, "and we agreed that it was time to end the unmanned aerial vehicle program," the mayor wrote in a statement. The drones were returned to the manufacturer.

The president says you can take out American citizens in foreign countries. . . . Well, if you can do that, you can take out somebody here as well.

Just days earlier, Charlottesville, Va., had become the first city in the country to pass a "no-drone zone" resolution, putting in place a two-year moratorium on the use of drones within Charlottesville limits.

"The big concern for us is that they're going to be everywhere," says John Whitehead, an attorney and president of The Rutherford Institute, a civil liberties organization in Charlottesville, which launched a preemptive fight against drones before the city council.

The move followed an Obama administration memo justifying the use of drones overseas to kill US citizens suspected of taking part in terrorist activities. "The president says you can take out American citizens in foreign countries," Mr. Whitehead says. "Well, if you can do that, you can take out somebody here as well."

On March 6, Attorney General Eric Holder may have reinforced such fears in testimony before the Senate Judiciary Committee when he refused to rule out the use of armed drones on US soil in an emergency "to protect the homeland."

If it all has an air of hysteria about it—Mr. Holder said there are no plans for the domestic use of armed drones and called the scenario "entirely hypothetical" and unlikely—privacy groups point to California's Alameda County, where officials insisted they wanted drones for search-and-rescue missions. An internal memo that surfaced from the sheriff's department, however, noted the drones could be used for "investigative and tactical surveillance, intelligence gathering, suspicious persons, and large crowd-control disturbances." The county dropped its plans.

The first and only known use of a drone in the arrest of a US citizen occurred in December 2011 in North Dakota, when the Nelson County Sheriff's Department asked to borrow one of the US Customs and Border Protection UAVs. The drone provided a good view of the three sons of the owner of a 3,000-acre farm who were involved in a standoff with law enforcement officers. As a result, police were able to tell that the brothers were unarmed, allowing them to enter the farm and arrest the brothers without the confrontation turning into a shootout.

Whitehead imagines a day when drones equipped with sound cannons, which release painful high-decibel sound waves that cause crowds to disperse, could be dispatched by the government to political protests and used as well to "effectively stifle free speech."

The concern that such technologies can be misused to invade privacy and suppress free speech "is a legitimate fear," says UND's Frazier. "Anytime we increase the technological capabilities of the government there's a justifiable concern there. But I think these fears can be offset by the fact that the drones we're using have very limited capabilities."

FAA regulations stipulate that weaponized drones cannot fly in unrestricted US airspace.

Nevertheless, privacy concerns are what have prompted groups including the nonprofit Electronic Frontier Foundation (EFF) to use the Freedom of Information Act to obtain hundreds of documents from the FAA outlining who has been requesting to use drones in America's skies, and why.

Roughly 40 percent of the drone flight requests submitted to the FAA are from the US military. "They are flying drones pretty regularly—eight hours a day, five days a week—to train pilots so that they will be able to fly drones," says Jessica Lynch, a staff attorney for EFF.

These drones are equipped with infrared scanning capabilities and other surveillance gadgets. "Drones have quite a number of technologies on board, including thermal cameras and the ability to intercept communications," Ms. Lynch says. "If they are training pilots, they are training them in these surveillance tools."

FAA regulations stipulate that weaponized drones cannot fly in unrestricted US airspace. The agency also has specific parameters for law enforcement drones. Law enforcement groups, for example, must maintain visual contact with the drone at all times and must also fly at relatively low altitudes.

These are regulations with which the Grand Forks Sheriff's Department has become familiar in the three years since it began looking into using drones, first establishing an Unmanned Aerial Systems unit as part of the department and then applying for COAs to use the drones. The unit, which went fully operational Feb. 1, has conducted 250 simulated missions, but has yet to use a drone in an operation.

Certification tends to be a lengthy and arduous process, Frazier says, adding that there are also some parameters for usage that are meant to promote safety, but can make it tricky for law enforcement to do its jobs.

One provision, for example, is that the drones can fly only by day. Another early rule was that the police had to give 48 hours' notice if they were going to use the drones.

"It's tough to predict if there is going to be a fire tomorrow, or a bank robbery the day after tomorrow," he says. The department was able to convince the FAA to let it fly the drones on one-hour notice instead.

That said, Frazier understands the public's concerns about the use of drones. For that reason, Grand Forks established a 15-member committee—made up of one-third public safety officials, one-third UND faculty, and one-third community residents—to evaluate the use of drones and to troubleshoot questions and concerns of the public. Every law enforcement action involving the drones is to be reviewed by the committee.

Frazier told committee members that the department did not intend to ask for the ability to use the drones for covert surveillance. "We will not use them to, quote, spy on people," Frazier says. Even if that were the intention, he adds, "These small drones are not particularly robust platforms for covert surveillance. I think the public can't understand that my little UAV can only fly for 15 minutes, can't fly out of my line of sight, and can't fly in greater than 15-knot winds."

As technology becomes cheaper and easier to use, it's tempting to use it all the time.

Out of concern that average citizens could be filmed by sensors on the aircraft, one of the committee's first acts was to instruct police to post road signs warning the public when UAVs are in use.

Yet some of the conversations EFF's Lynch has had with other law enforcement agencies haven't been as reassuring about privacy, she says. "We've talked to police about this, and they've said, 'Well, we're going to fly the drones in public airspace, and if you walk around in public you don't have an expectation of privacy in your movements.'

"While that might be true for a police officer following you down the street, I don't know if that applies when a drone can fly over and surveil everybody walking down that street for an extended period of time," Lynch says.

"You can make the case that drones are helping law enforcement better do their jobs for less [cost] and we should incorporate it," she adds. "As technology becomes cheaper and easier to use, it's tempting to use it all the time."

That is the fear of Texas state lawmaker Lance Gooden, who in February proposed some of the toughest anti-drone legislation in the country. It would prevent drone operators from collecting images, sounds, and smells—or hovering over any home—without permission.

"Two to four years from now, it'll be impossible to get legislation passed because every law enforcement agency will want drones," says Mr. Gooden. While the drone lobby is growing, it is not as powerful as it will become, he adds.

Currently, his bill has the support of 101 of the 150 members of the state Legislature. But some longtime drone experts say such laws are overkill and could impede growth of technology that is useful and relatively inexpensive.

"The ordinances that have been passed are absolutely absurd," says retired Lt. Gen. David Deptula, the first deputy chief of staff for Intelligence, Reconnaissance, and Surveillance for the US Air Force. "And what's precluded are the very valuable civilian applications in terms of traffic control, firefighting, disaster response, border security, the monitoring of power lines—the list goes on and on."

As for privacy concerns, "I can't think of another way of saying it, but that they are unfounded," Deptula adds. "All you have to do is look up in any major metropolitan city and see the cameras all around. And have they ever heard of satellites? Where do they think Google maps come from?"

Frazier concurs. People with a good zoom lens have better cameras than do his small drones, he adds, pointing out that one of the Grand Forks Sheriff's Department's drones has a simple off-the-shelf Panasonic.

The average GPS-enabled cellphone can now track people and their movements to within a few feet, he notes.

That said, "I understand what people mean when they say it's 'creepy,'" Frazier says. "I value my privacy as much as anyone does—it's very sacred in this country." Even if they could do it legally, law enforcement agencies would be making a big mistake using drones for covert surveillance—for the time being, he adds.

"It would be a fatal mistake at this point. We really need to take a crawl, walk, run approach. To go to covert surveillance brings us to a run," Frazier says of the law enforcement community. "If that means we're not Buck Rogers in the 21st century, we're comfortable with that."

12

How Stores Spy on You

ShopSmart

ShopSmart magazine and ShopSmart.org are nonprofit consumer research and publishing organizations within the Consumer Reports family of services.

Most American shoppers don't realize it, but they are being closely watched as they make their way through the aisles of their favorite stores—and it's not to prevent shoplifting. It is to gather data about their shopping habits and about them personally. Just a few of the common techniques include in-store Wi-Fi systems that latch on to customers' cell phones to track and time their movement through a store; video cameras that couple with face-recognition software to identify individual shoppers and analyze their moods and preferences; and pin-hole cameras in product shelves or video ad screens that are watching shoppers right back. The information gathered in this way is big business for the retail industry but represents a significant privacy threat for consumers. The Consumer Privacy Bill of Rights is a good step toward addressing this issue.

We're used to being watched when we shop. Cookies track our every move online, and salespeople follow us around high-end stores. But many walk-in retailers are taking spying to a new level.

Video cameras record your every move. Your face and car's license plate are captured and filed in searchable databases. Hidden cameras classify you by age, sex, and ethnicity, and even detect your body language and mood. Even your bank account records are being pried into. The main goal of these surveillance methods, of course, is to get you to shop more and spend more.

If all of this is news to you, it's probably because disclosure is poor to nonexistent, say experts familiar with these practices. Also, odds are you've never read or decoded what you've agreed to in bank, retailer, and app privacy policies. And you probably never imagined that retailers would be so interested in spying on honest shoppers. "While most consumers understand a need for security cameras, few expect that the in-store video advertising monitor they're watching . . . is watching them" with a pinhole camera, says Pam Dixon, executive director of World Privacy Forum, a nonprofit research group in San Diego.

With facial-recognition software, your mug shot can be captured and digitally filed without your knowledge or permission.

Some stores now have cameras in their dressing rooms so you can more easily check the fit of your jeans from the rear, but they also collect details about you and your shopping habits.

All of this tracking is a mixed bag for shoppers. When a store closely monitors operations to improve its service, that's a win-win. But when retailers intrude on your privacy with little or no explanation of what they're doing or how they use your info, that's just plain sneaky. Here's what's going on in many stores around the U.S. and what you need to know.

Video Cameras Inside and Out

High-resolution video cameras monitor all areas in and outside the store. The footage is then stored and catalogued for easy searching. With facial-recognition software, your mug shot can be captured and digitally filed without your knowledge or permission. Ditto for your car's license plate.

What's creepy about them: Gaze trackers are hidden in tiny holes in the shelving and detect which brands you're looking at and how long for each. There are even mannequins whose eyes are cameras that detect the age, sex, ethnicity, and facial expressions of passers-by.

The video can be merged with a store's other data, such as footage of you at the cash register plus the transaction details of what you bought, for how much, using what credit card. Your face and vehicle license plate can be linked. If that info is not securely stored, it could be hacked. Stores don't provide sufficient disclosure, so you can't opt out to protect your privacy. Last October [2012], the Federal Trade Commission recommended clear disclosure to consumers, security standards for stored video, and customer opt-out or consent in certain circumstances.

What's in it for you: Stores use video customer counts to set staffing and reduce cashier-line backups. The system can also nab shoplifters and identity thieves and examine the veracity of slip-and-fall injury claims, keeping fraud costs (and prices) down.

Who's using them: "Most of the big chains are trying video analytics," says Robert Hetu, research director for retailing at Gartner, an investment research firm. But retailers want their own privacy. Macy's, for example, employs video analytics, according to printed promotional materials from Cisco, a maker of such systems, but a Macy's spokeswoman didn't return our repeated calls for comment. A Target spokesperson refused to comment about the store's use of video analytics and other tools, even though its privacy policy states that the retailer collects information "recorded by in-store cameras."

Mobile Phones Reveal Your Location

Your mobile phone is an excellent device for tracking your shopping route. So retailers and malls are beginning to monitor all visitors' cell signals, which help create "heat maps" that glow red where the most foot traffic is—perfect for showing where to best place displays, in-store ads, and high-margin merchandise. The retailer tracking systems can identify individual shoppers by monitoring your phone's International Mobile Subscriber Identity number (constantly transmitted from all cell phones to their service providers) or Media Access Control address (transmitted when the device's Wi-Fi is enabled, which is the default setting on most devices). That phone ID lets stores know when you shop—not just today but also every day your ID signal comes back in range.

Research shows consumers don't trust retailers with their personal information, but if an attractive offer is made, they will give it.

What's creepy about it: Cisco the technology giant, is testing a system at an undisclosed store. It automatically detects your mobile device and connects you to the retailer's free Wi-Fi network. "Once the customer gets on the network, he has opted in, and the privacy concerns are allayed," says Sujai Hejela, general manager of Cisco's wireless networking group.

That allows the retailer to keep you on the store's network, which can also detect when you search other online sellers for lower prices. "The retailer is not controlling but is managing the flow of information, and the shopper sees the retail brand as helping her shop," says Jon Stine, director of Internet business solutions at Cisco. That's not necessarily bad for shoppers. For example, if you check prices online while you're in the store, you might get messages that the store will match the lower prices you find.

What's in it for you: Stores can use the information to improve service. Also, you can get coupons and discounts. "Our research shows consumers don't trust retailers with their personal information, but if an attractive offer is made, they will give it," Hetu says.

Who's using it: Lots of retailers and malls have Wi-Fi networks.

Video Ads Are Watching You

When you look at onscreen video ads, they might be looking right back at you. Tiny pinhole cameras can be built into the monitor. Facial-detection technology determines your age group, sex, ethnicity, and maybe even your mood, so it can serve up a message targeted to you. And radio-frequency identification (RFID) tags placed on the merchandise detect when you pick up an item. They can trigger a nearby digital sign to feed you targeted ads or details about the product. Kiosks and interactive touch screens often do the same thing.

What's creepy about it: Not only are stores doing little or nothing to disclose that signs are watching you, but some privacy advocates also fear that the technology also could be used for discriminatory pricing based on age, sex, or ethnicity.

What's in it for you: Ads can be more targeted to your needs.

Who's using it: Vendors, analysts, and critics say big retail chains commonly use digital signage, but the stores we checked either denied it or didn't respond to our inquiry.

Returns and Exchanges

Stores have been monitoring and tracking returns and exchanges for years to identify and prevent the 1 percent that are fraudulent. Now some stores are rewarding the honest 99 percent of customers who return items with special offers—say, a 20 percent discount or $10 off a specific item—to encourage them to spend their refund in the store.

[Privacy] rights are constantly evolving as technology finds new ways to pry into your affairs and consumer advocates push back with new protections.

What's creepy about it: The reward is designed to appeal to you, based on statistical models that predict consumer behavior. It's usually valid for only 1 to 2 hours, so you're pressured to use it or lose it. The offers work to serve the retailer's needs—as a result, the deals might be on stuff that's about to be marked down for clearance anyway, or for a brand that you don't usually prefer.

What's in it for you: Money-saving opportunities, if you can resist buying stuff you don't need.

Who's using them: The Retail Equation, which markets the system to stores, did not return our repeated phone calls.

Shoppers Have Rights

Privacy rights spring from a mishmash of implicit and explicit language in the U.S. Constitution, some state constitutions, state and federal laws, court rulings, and contracts between businesses and consumers. Those rights are constantly evolving as technology finds new ways to pry into your affairs and consumer advocates push back with new protections. Last year [2013], the [Barack] Obama administration neatly framed the matter into a Consumer Privacy Bill of Rights proposal. The main provisions would give consumers:

- The right to control how a company collects, uses, and discloses your data to others and the option of giving, withdrawing, or limiting your consent.

- Up-front explanation of what data is being collected, why, what users will do with it, how long they'll store it, and whom they'll share it with.

- A requirement that users protect consumer data from hackers, thieves, and other unauthorized parties.

- The ability to see and correct the information being collected and stored.

It's just a proposal at this point. We think it's a very good start. But you should also protect your own privacy. Always read privacy policies on retailers' websites. Also read the permissions you're asked to give to an app before you download it to your phone. Be sure to recheck those policies periodically.

We recently took another look at the privacy policy of Shopkick, an app that we've written about in the past, and found that it was updated in December [2013]. Shopkick is an example of a rewards program with a privacy trade-off. It lets you earn rewards, called kicks, just for walking into participating stores. More than 7,500 retailers are in on the action, including Crate & Barrel, Old Navy, and Target. You can redeem kicks for freebies such as a Starbucks latte, movie tickets, and even a designer handbag. Nice perks! But the app's privacy policy reveals that it collects stores visited, items purchased, Internet search terms used, date of birth, and much more. That's a big trade-off. Is it worth it? Think about that question before you sign up.

13

Domestic Surveillance Is Bad for the US Economy

Hugo Miller

Hugo Miller is a reporter for Bloomberg News in Toronto, Canada.

The recently publicized details about extensive US domestic surveillance programs, such as the National Security Agency's (NSA) widespread collection of phone-call data, has made some businesses distrustful of basing their operations in the United States. Instead of choosing to locate their firms in US cities, some companies are instead choosing to locate in places like Canada, which has stronger protections for the privacy of data. Domestic surveillance is bad for the US economy because it is driving away business that could cost the country as much as $35 billion in losses through 2016.

In the British Columbia town of Kamloops, arid as a desert with cool summer nights, Telus Corp. only has to turn on the air conditioning about 40 hours a year to keep its computer servers from overheating.

The chilly temperatures are part of Canadian companies' sales pitch to businesses looking for places to store their growing troves of digital information as cheaply as possible. They also boast of inexpensive hydroelectric power and low seismic activity. And now they're touting what they say is a new advantage: less snooping.

Hugo Miller, "NSA Spying Sends Data Clients North of the Border," Bloomberg.com, January 9, 2014. Reproduced by permission.

Revelations that the U.S. National Security Agency [NSA] has spied on data networks run by American companies have given Canadian data-center operators an opportunity. They're telling customers from Europe and Asia that laws north of the border are more protective of privacy. Sales of storage services in Canada are growing 20 percent a year at Telus and Rogers Communications Inc. U.S.-based technology companies, meanwhile, complain that the NSA scandal has hurt their business.

"There is a structural advantage in Canada in that the data is here and the privacy protection is more stringent," said Lloyd Switzer, who runs Telus's network of data centers.

International outrage over NSA surveillance may cost U.S. companies as much as $35 billion in lost revenue through 2016.

The company has 10 data centers in Quebec, Ontario, Alberta and British Columbia, where it opened a [Canadian] C$75 million, 215,000-square-foot (20,000-square-meter) facility in Kamloops last year. That site has room for six more modules of expansion, which would increase the investment into the hundreds of millions of dollars.

Snowden's Revelation

Data privacy came under scrutiny in the U.S. in June [2013] after former NSA contractor Edward Snowden revealed that his employer was monitoring phone and e-mail traffic emanating from the U.S.

International outrage over NSA surveillance may cost U.S. companies as much as $35 billion in lost revenue through 2016, according to the Information Technology & Innovation Foundation, a policy research group in Washington [DC] whose board includes representatives of companies such as International Business Machines Corp. and Intel Corp.

Rogers, which competes with Telus for phone and Internet customers, gets about C$70 million ([US]$66 million) in annual revenue from data storage—still tiny at less than 1 percent of total sales. The unit has had more inquiries in the past 12 months from companies outside North America than in the entire previous decade, A.J. Byers, who heads up the business, said in an interview.

Overseas Demand

"A lot of international companies trying to gain access to the U.S. used to go directly to the U.S.," Byers said. "Now we see a lot of European and Asian companies talking to us."

Rogers and Telus are looking to capitalize on the surge in demand for data storage to make up for the slowing growth of smartphones, which more than half of Canadians already have. Stock gains for the companies also have slowed. Shares of Rogers climbed 6 percent last year after gaining 15 percent in 2012. Telus rose 12 percent last year, its smallest annual increase in four years.

Last month [December 2013], a U.S. federal judge ruled that the NSA probably acted illegally in collecting telephone-call data, allowing a lawsuit to go forward claiming the practice violates the U.S. Constitution.

U.S. District Judge William H. Pauley III in Manhattan [New York] late last month ruled the NSA's bulk collection of phone records is legal, challenging the earlier ruling. The NSA has said it's pleased with Pauley's decision.

Facing Charges

Snowden has been charged with theft and espionage by the U.S. government and has avoided arrest by remaining in Russia. While editorials in newspapers such as the *New York Times* have recommended that he get clemency, Janet Napolitano, the former head of the Department of Homeland Security, has said he doesn't deserve a reprieve.

Canada's Privacy Act, enacted in 1983, imposes obligations on 250 federal-government departments and agencies to limit collection and use of personal information, and gives citizens the right to access that data and correct mistakes.

Still, the data-center sales pitch glosses over the long history of intelligence-sharing between Canada and the U.S. The governments have collaborated as far back as the 1940s, said Ron Deibert, an Internet-security expert who runs the University of Toronto's Citizen Lab.

"Anyone who would look to Canada as a safe haven would be fooling themselves," Deibert said in a phone interview. "Canada would be one of the poorest choices as we have a long-standing relationship with the NSA."

Surveillance Allowed

Communications Security Establishment [CSE], the country's intelligence agency for communications and electronics, is forbidden from monitoring purely domestic traffic. Surveillance of foreign communications that involve someone in Canada may be authorized, as long as one of the parties is outside the country—a rule established after the Sept. 11 [2001] terrorist attacks.

Canada's data-protection rules . . . go well beyond U.S. regulations and make Canada a natural place for companies to store clients' data.

CSE works with its Five Eyes information-gathering partners—the U.S., U.K. [United Kingdom], Australia and New Zealand—and must comply with Canadian law in its interactions with them, Andrew McLaughlin, a spokesman for the agency, said by e-mail.

A CSE commissioner, typically a retired judge, submits an annual report to Canada's Parliament through the defense ministry. Justice Robert Decary, who did the last such report in June, wrote that he was "deeply disappointed" that legislative amendments to Canada's National Defense Act proposed by his predecessors that "would improve the provisions that were hastily enacted in the aftermath of September 2001" haven't yet been adopted.

"Respecting Privacy"

"CSE collects foreign signals intelligence to support government decision-making for national security, defense and international affairs," Adrian Simpson, another spokesman for the Ottawa-based agency, said by e-mail. "We do so in accordance with Government of Canada intelligence priorities, respecting the privacy of Canadians and Canadian laws in all activities."

Canada's data-protection rules still go well beyond U.S. regulations and make Canada a natural place for companies to store clients' data, said Solium Capital Inc. Chief Executive Officer Michael Broadfoot. His company, which helps firms such as Barclays Plc manage their employee stock-options programs, stores data in Telus's center in Calgary, the city at the foot of the Rockies where Solium is based.

"We're able to generally host so far anybody in the world from Canadian locations," said Broadfoot. "We would not be able to do that from U.S. locations. Canada's privacy laws are a gold standard."

14

Technology Drives Advances in Domestic Surveillance

Steven Kurlander

Steven Kurlander is an attorney and political communications specialist in Monticello, New York. He blogs at Kurly's Kommentary, Huffington Post, *and* Florida Squeeze.

The capabilities of domestic surveillance have expanded rapidly in recent years because of the equally rapid spread of new technologies that facilitate information gathering. However, many of the same technological innovations that drive the government's surveillance programs are also available to consumers. Everyday Americans can already buy sophisticated surveillance gear such as remote-viewing security camera systems, global positioning system (GPS) trackers, even unmanned aerial vehicles—known as drones. The unprecedented proliferation of such technologies necessitates stronger privacy protections and safeguards, not just to regulate government entities that may employ them, but to limit the personal use of spying equipment by citizens against each other.

Spy technology continues to become ever more sophisticated—and deadly too. That's sparked a major debate about how domestic spying should be limited to ensure constitutional safeguards of US citizens. And while it is indeed a very important discussion to be had in terms of limiting a

Steven Kurlander, "Domestic Surveillance: Spy vs. Spy, American vs. American," *Huffington Post* Blog, March 13, 2013. www.huffingtonpost.com/the-blog. Reproduced by permission.

fresh wave of unrestrained government intrusion into our private lives, Congress may want to also start talking about how far American citizens should be allowed to spy on each other too.

There's been a corresponding boom surge in the use of cheap, technological spying equipment that Americans buy and use to tract and gather information on one another.

You don't need a drone. For a few hundred dollars, you can now buy sophisticated surveillance tools to gather information you once paid thousands a day to private investigators to spy on targeted individuals.

We've become a nation where every movement we make and every communication we engage in can be easily tracked by the government, the cell phone provider—and each other.

Watching Main Street

We walk Main Streets and drive thoroughfares that are monitored by cameras and speed passes. We work at computer terminals that allow our bosses to monitor our behavior and work productivity, minute by minute—and we use social media and search engines that can track our usage and establish personality profiles to sell and share.

US Department of Homeland Security recently was reported to have customized Predator drones to carry out such home surveillance tasks as identifying American citizens who are carrying guns and tracking their cell phones.

And we now also routinely spy on our families and one another too in our homes, businesses, and elsewhere, simply [by] clandestinely hiding spy cameras or affixing and monitoring GPS [global positioning system] monitors to phones, computers, vehicles or possessions.

"It's truly a case of spy vs. spy when parents keep [track] of kids, neighbors can keep tabs on the goings on around their home and spouses can detect infidelity with a spy cam or GPS tracker," says Dan Iacono, who owns DynaSpy Security, Inc., which sells an array of sophisticated spying equipment at two very busy stores in Long Island [New York] and Fort Lauderdale [Florida]. He describes his business as "booming."

Recently, the use of sophisticated spy equipment has mainly centered on the use of unmanned drones, also known as unmanned aerial vehicles (UAVs), on US soil by both the military and police agencies alike.

Drones on US Soil

US Department of Homeland Security recently was reported to have customized Predator drones to carry out such home surveillance tasks as identifying American citizens who are carrying guns and tracking their cell phones. In response, the House of Representatives passed legislation this month [March 2013] demanding that the Department of Defense disclose whether in fact military drones are tracking US citizens on American soil.

And of course, there was Senator Rand Paul of Kentucky, standing on his feet for 13 hours in the Senate, filibustering the nomination of John Brennan as director of the CIA [Central Intelligence Agency], arguing that due process rights of Americans were at stake if Brennan and the [Barack] Obama Administration were allowed to use such drones to kill on US soil American citizens alleged to be traitors—like Anwar al-Awlaki, the American who was droned in Yemen in September, 2011.

Oregon Senator Ron Wyden, who was the only Democrat to join the Kentucky senator know for his libertarian views in his filibuster, stated last week that the Paul filibuster may have been [a] decisive moment on the drone issue and due process concerns as well and that a new, bipartisan "checks and balances" caucus would be forming in Congress.

"Checks and Balances"

But those "checks and balances" need to be formulated not in terms of due process and drone killings, but also to deal [with] ensuring that Americans can have some semblance of privacy in all aspects of their lives in a digital age that promotes and encompasses the collection of personal information by more than the government, some of which should be just plain personally secret.

The right and necessity of secrecy is just not within the purview of government, but is an elementary privacy right that our founding fathers recognized as an important tenet of a democratic society that allows Americans to safeguard mistakes, beliefs, and errant behavior not from Washington, but from one another.

Practically speaking, we are in the midst of a new age of privacy deprivation, where it's almost impossible to run away and hide, to gain total solitude, or even attain basic privacy from the outside world.

Even if Paul and others in Congress push for new safeguards [that] are established to limit the executive branch's reach into the personal lives of Americans, such "checks and balances" need to apply to limiting our personal use of spying equipment against one another too.

15

The American Public Is Skeptical of Domestic Surveillance

Pew Research Center for the People & the Press

The Pew Research Center for the People & the Press is one of seven programs operated by the Pew Research Center, a nonpartisan, nonprofit research organization that seeks to inform the public about the issues, attitudes, and trends shaping America and the world.

According to a poll by the Pew Research Center in January 2014, 53 percent of the American public disapproved of the government's collection of telephone and Internet data as part of its antiterrorism efforts, a figure that jumped nearly 10 percent in just six months. Nearly half of the respondents also said there were not adequate limits on what kind of information could be collected by the government. A speech given by President Barack Obama on reforms to protect civil liberties in connection with domestic surveillance did little to allay the public's skepticism on the issue, with surveys done in the days both before and after the president's speech showing little difference.

President [Barack] Obama's speech on Friday [January 17, 2014] outlining changes to the National Security Agency's [NSA] collection of telephone and internet data did not register widely with the public. Half say they have heard nothing at all about his proposed changes to the NSA, and another 41% say they heard only a little bit. Even among those [who] heard about Obama's speech, few think the changes will improve privacy protections, or make it more difficult for the government to fight terrorism.

The new national survey by the Pew Research Center and *USA Today*, conducted Jan. 15–19 among 1,504 adults, finds that overall approval of the program has declined since last summer [2013], when the story first broke based on [former NSA contractor] Edward Snowden's leaked information.

Today, 40% approve of the government's collection of telephone and internet data as part of anti-terrorism efforts, while 53% disapprove. In July, more Americans approved (50%) than disapproved (44%) of the program.

In addition, nearly half (48%) say there are not adequate limits on what telephone and internet data the government can collect; fewer (41%) say there are adequate limits on the government's data collection. About four-in-ten Republicans (39%) and independents (38%)—and about half of Democrats (48%)—think there are adequate limits on the information that the government can collect.

> *Democrats remain more supportive of the NSA surveillance program than Republicans, though support is down across party lines.*

Reflecting the limited impact of Obama's address, overall approval of the program and opinions about whether adequate safeguards are in place were no different in three nights of interviewing conducted after the speech (Jan. 17–19) than during the two nights of interviewing conducted prior to the address (Jan. 15–16).

Overall, the public is divided about whether Edward Snowden's leak of classified information, which brought the program to light, has served or harmed the public interest:

45% say it has served the public interest while 43% say it harmed it. Nonetheless, a 56% majority wants to see the government pursue a criminal case against Snowden, while 32% oppose this. This is little changed from June, shortly after Snowden's first leaks of information about the program.

Democrats Divided over Surveillance Program

Democrats remain more supportive of the NSA surveillance program than Republicans, though support is down across party lines. Today, Democrats are divided (46% approve, 48% disapprove) in their view of the program. Last June, they approved by a 20-point margin (58% vs. 38%).

Republicans now disapprove of the program by a 56% to 37% margin. Approval is down eight points among Republicans from 45% last June. There continues to be a substantial divide within the Republican base: Republicans and Republican leaners who agree with the Tea Party are overwhelmingly opposed to the NSA program, while those who do not identify with the Tea Party are more divided.

The decline in approval of the NSA surveillance program spans most demographic groups, though the drop in support is particularly evident among minority groups. Last June, 60% of both blacks and Hispanics approved of the government's surveillance program. That has fallen to 43% among blacks and 40% among Hispanics today. Among whites, 39% approve of the program today, little changed from 44% in June.

NSA Changes Have Little Impact

Obama's proposed changes to the NSA's data collection program did not register widely with the public. Just 49% say they heard about the proposed changes, with little difference across partisan groups.

Among those that did hear about the proposals, large majorities of Republicans (86%) and independents (78%) say these changes will not make much difference when it comes to protecting people's privacy. Among Democrats who have heard of the changes, 56% say they won't make much difference.

There is little concern that the changes to the NSA's surveillance activities will hurt the government's ability to fight terrorism. Overall, 79% of those who have heard about the proposals say they won't make much difference in the government's ability to fight terrorism; this view is shared by 85% of independents, 77% of Democrats and 75% of Republicans.

Prosecute Snowden, but Public Split on Impact of Leak

The public is split on whether Edward Snowden's leaks served the public interest, with 45% saying they did and 43% saying the leaks harmed public interest. But by 56% to 32%, most think that the government should pursue a criminal case against Snowden. These opinions are largely unchanged from last June, when Snowden first disclosed classified information to news organizations.

While most of the public wants the government to pursue a criminal case against Snowden, young people offer the least support for his prosecution.

There is a large age gap when it comes to views of the NSA revelations and the public interest. More adults ages 50 and older believe that the leaks harmed the public interest (49%) than served the public interest (37%). Among adults 18–29, sentiment is reversed, with 57% saying Snowden served the public interest and 35% saying he harmed it.

There are no significant differences on this issue by party, as both Republicans and Democrats are divided.

Those who attended college are more likely than those who didn't to see the leaks as serving the public interest. About half of college graduates (49%) and those with some college experience (51%) say this, compared with 38% of those with no more than a high school degree.

While most of the public wants the government to pursue a criminal case against Snowden, young people offer the least support for his prosecution.

Those younger than 30 are divided, with 42% wanting a criminal case against Snowden and 42% saying the government should not pursue one. Support for prosecution is much higher among those 50 and older, who think the government should pursue a case by more than two-to-one.

Both Democrats (62%–27%) and Republicans (54%–28%) think the government should pursue a criminal case. About half of independents (51%) want a criminal case against Snowden, while four-in-ten (39%) say the government should not pursue one.

Fully 70% of those who approve of the government's surveillance program favor Snowden's prosecution. Those who disapprove of the program are divided: 45% say the government should pursue a criminal case against Snowden while 43% are opposed.

Obama Job Rating

Barack Obama's job approval rating has shown little change from last month. In the current survey, 49% disapprove of how he is handling his job and 43% approve. Obama's ratings had steadily declined from May to November of last year, before he regained some ground in December.

In the last month, there have been no significant changes in partisan approval. About three-quarters of Democrats (77%) approve and 17% disapprove; among Republicans, 12%

approve and 84% disapprove. Independents, on balance, continue to view his job performance negatively—37% approve and 53% disapprove.

Organizations to Contact

The editors have compiled the following list of organizations concerned with the issues debated in this book. The descriptions are derived from materials provided by the organizations. All have publications or information available for interested readers. The list was compiled on the date of publication of the present volume; names, addresses, phone and fax numbers, and e-mail and Internet addresses may change. Be aware that many organizations take several weeks or longer to respond to inquiries, so allow as much time as possible.

American Civil Liberties Union (ACLU)
125 Broad St., 18th Floor, New York, NY 10004
(212) 549-2500
e-mail: info@aclu.org
website: www.aclu.org

Through activism in courts, legislatures, and communities nationwide, the American Civil Liberties Union works to defend and preserve the individual rights and liberties that the Constitution and laws of the United States guarantee to everyone. The ACLU has been a key player in the effort to stop the National Security Agency's (NSA) mass warrantless collection of e-mails, phone calls, and customer records of ordinary Americans. The ACLU website has an extensive collection of reports, briefings, blogs, and news updates related to domestic surveillance programs, civil rights, privacy, and the freedom of speech and expression in electronic media. Reports available on the ACLU website include "Civil Liberties in the Digital Age" and "Protecting Privacy from Aerial Surveillance: Recommendations for Government Use of Drone Aircraft."

Cato Institute
1000 Massachusetts Ave. NW, Washington, DC 20001-5403
(202) 842-0200 • fax: (202) 842-3490
website: www.cato.org

The Cato Institute is a libertarian public policy research foundation dedicated to limiting the role of government, protecting individual liberties, and promoting free markets. The organization's website features a variety of publications related to domestic surveillance and a special section of the site titled "NSA Abuses" hosts a collection of selected commentary and videos from around the web as well as from Cato's own writers. Among Cato's regular publications are the quarterly magazine *Regulation*, the bimonthly *Cato Policy Report*, and the periodic *Cato Journal*.

Center for Democracy and Technology (CDT)

1634 I St. NW, #1100, Washington, DC   20006
(202) 637-9800 • fax: (202) 637-0968
website: www.cdt.org

The Center for Democracy and Technology is a nonprofit public interest organization that works to keep the Internet open, innovative, and free. As a civil liberties group with expertise in law, technology, and policy, CDT advocates for free expression and privacy in communications technologies and works to find practical and innovative solutions to public policy challenges while protecting civil liberties. The CDT's *Global Policy Weekly* blog highlights the latest Internet policy developments and proposals from around the world, and the CDT website features regular news updates about security and surveillance issues, including the National Security Agency's ongoing data collection program.

Electronic Frontier Foundation (EFF)

454 Shotwell St., San Francisco, CA   94110-1914
(415) 436-9333 • fax: (415) 436-9993
e-mail: info@eff.org
website: www.eff.org

The Electronic Frontier Foundation is an international nonprofit digital rights advocacy and legal organization. The group works to raise public awareness about civil liberties and computer-based communications, educate policymakers and the public about issues that underlie free and open communications, and support litigation in the public interest to preserve, protect, and extend First Amendment rights in the digital world. The EFF has been a key player in the effort to stop the National Security Agency's mass warrantless collection of e-mails, phone calls, and customer records of ordinary Americans. The EFF website features information about the group's various projects and initiatives as well as white papers, legal case documents, and press releases. Its regularly updated *Deeplinks* blog features posts on electronic communications, privacy, censorship, regulation, free expression, and activism. A section of the EFF website devoted to privacy issues features an extensive archive of information related to domestic surveillance in its many forms.

First Amendment Coalition (FAC)

534 4th St., Suite B, San Rafael, CA 94901
(415) 460-5060 • fax: (415) 460-5155
website: www.firstamendmentcoalition.org

Founded in 1988, the First Amendment Coalition is a nonprofit public interest organization dedicated to advancing free speech, open and accountable government, and public participation in civic affairs. The Coalition acts locally, statewide, and nationally by offering free legal consultations for anyone frustrated in the exercise of their First Amendment rights; strategic litigation to enhance First Amendment freedoms; educational and informational programs offered online, in books and in conferences; legislative oversight; and public advocacy through writings of op-eds and public speaking. The FAC website includes dozens of items related to domestic surveillance, privacy, and civil rights. Recent articles of interest include "The Connection Between Drone Strikes and Massive Government Surveillance Programs" and "For Google, Facebook et al, the Best Defense Against NSA Surveillance Is Not Legal Reform, but Technology That Forces the Agency to Come Through the 'Front Door.'" The FAC site also maintains an extensive law library of leading court decisions in the areas of freedom of information and freedom of speech.

Heritage Foundation

214 Massachusetts Ave. NE, Washington, DC   20002-4999
(202) 546-4400
website: www.heritage.org

The Heritage Foundation is a conservative think tank that works to create and advocate for public policies that promote the ideals of free enterprise, limited government, individual freedom, traditional American values, and a strong national defense. The organization's website includes dozens of issue briefs, research papers, commentaries, blog posts, and infographics related to domestic surveillance topics, such as the National Security Agency (NSA), NSA leaker Edward Snowden, and the use of drones. Publications available online include "Phone Records and the NSA: Legal and Keeping America Safe," "Snowden Is a Traitor in All but Name," and "Holding Back Progress Is a Fool's Errand: Drones Are Coming."

National Security Agency (NSA)

9800 Savage Rd., Fort Meade, MD   20755-6152
(301) 688-6524 • fax: (301) 688-6198
e-mail: nsapao@nsa.gov
website: www.nsa.gov

The National Security Agency is the federal intelligence agency responsible for the global monitoring, collection, decoding, translation, and analysis of information for foreign intelligence and counterintelligence purposes. The NSA has two main divisions, the Signals Intelligence Directorate (SID) and the Information Assurance Directorate (IAD). SID gathers, analyzes, and disseminates intelligence information from foreign signals. IAD prevents foreign adversaries from accessing classified information. The NSA's website offers extensive information about the agency's leadership, mission, vision, and values as well as many of its past and present programs and interests. FAQs, research reports, transcripts of speeches and testimonies, and a variety of other resources. The NSA website also houses a collection of documents related to cryptology and the agency operates the Center for Cryptologic History.

The NSA publishes the quarterly electronic magazine *The Next Wave*, which focuses on technical advancements and research activities in telecommunications and information technologies.

New America Foundation

1899 L St. NW, Suite 400, Washington, DC   20036
(202) 986-2700 • fax: (202) 986-3696
website: www.newamerica.net

The New America Foundation is a nonprofit, nonpartisan public policy institute that invests in new thinkers and new ideas to address the next generation of challenges facing the United States. New America supports municipal broadband and publishes articles and policy papers on the Internet. Its website features a variety of articles about domestic surveillance, privacy, and civil rights, including more than one thousand items that mention the National Security Agency. Of particular note is the January 2014 report, "Do NSA's Bulk Surveillance Programs Help Stop Terrorism?"

Office of the Director of National Intelligence (ODNI)

Office of the Director of National Intelligence
Washington, DC   20511
(703) 733-8600
website: www.dni.gov

The Office of the Director of National Intelligence began operations in April 2005 and is responsible for overseeing and coordinating the activities of sixteen other intelligence agencies and organizations that work both independently and collaboratively to gather and analyze the intelligence necessary for foreign relations and national security activities. Among the agencies under its purview are the National Security Agency (NSA), Central Intelligence Agency (CIA), Federal Bureau of Investigation (FBI), and Department of Homeland Security (DHS). The ODNI website is a good resource for learning about the US intelligence community, how it is structured, what roles its various agencies play, and how they work together.

Pew Research Center

1615 L St. NW, Suite 700, Washington, DC   20036
(202) 419-4300 • fax: (202) 419-4349
website: www.pewresearch.org

Pew Research Center is a nonpartisan research organization that informs the public about the issues, attitudes, and trends shaping America and the world. It conducts public opinion polling, demographic research, media content analysis, and other empirical social science research. Pew Research does not take policy positions. It is a subsidiary of the Pew Charitable Trusts, an independent nonprofit research organization. The Pew Research Center has extensively studied various aspects of domestic surveillance and its website features a wide variety of fact sheets, reports, and studies, including the publications "Balancing Act: National Security and Civil Liberties in Post-9/11 Era" and "Americans Divided on Whether Drones Make US Safer."

US Senate

Senate Office Building, Washington, DC   20510
(202) 224-3121
website: www.senate.gov

The Senate is the upper house of the United States' bicameral legislature in Washington, DC. Along with the House of Representatives, it comprises the United States Congress. One of the Senate's functions is to create bills and get them approved as laws by both houses of Congress. The US Senate's website includes nearly six thousand documents related to the National Security Agency (NSA), ranging from transcripts of congressional testimony and statements about the NSA by individual senators, intelligence officials, and members of the public, to news updates and information about the many legislative efforts related to the NSA's gathering of communications records. The Senate website includes thousands of other documents related to domestic surveillance, drones, and NSA leaker Edward Snowden. Contact information for individual senators is also available on the site.

The White House

1600 Pennsylvania Ave. NW, Washington, DC   20500
(202) 456-1111
website: www.whitehouse.gov

Whitehouse.gov is the official website of US president Barack Obama. Resources available from the site related to domestic surveillance include a variety of presidential statements and the text of speeches about the National Security Agency, domestic surveillance, privacy, and civil rights. Also available is the December 2013 report by the president's review group on intelligence and communications technologies titled "Liberty and Security in a Changing World," which sets forth forty-six recommendations designed to protect national security and advance US foreign policy while respecting privacy and civil liberties.

Bibliography

Books

Julia Angwin   *Dragnet Nation: A Quest for Privacy, Security and Freedom in a World of Relentless Surveillance.* New York: Times Books, 2014.

Heidi Boghosian   *Spying on Democracy: Government Surveillance, Corporate Power and Public Resistance.* San Francisco: City Lights, 2013.

David Brin   *The Transparent Society: Will Technology Force Us to Choose Between Technology and Freedom?* Cambridge, MA: Basic Books, 1998.

Ronald J. Deibert   *Black Code: Surveillance, Privacy, and the Dark Side of the Internet.* Toronto, Canada: Signal, 2013.

Christian Fuchs et al., eds.   *Internet and Surveillance: The Challenges of Web 2.0 and Social Media.* New York: Routledge, 2012.

Louise Gerdes   *At Issue: Drones.* Farmington Hills, MI: Greenhaven, 2014.

Glenn Greenwald   *No Place to Hide: Edward Snowden, the NSA, and the U.S. Surveillance State.* New York: Metropolitan, 2014.

Luke Harding   *The Snowden Files: The Inside Story of the World's Most Wanted Man.* New York: Vintage, 2014.

Shane Harris   *The Watchers: The Rise of America's*
                      Surveillance State. London, United
                      Kingdom: Penguin, 2011.

Sean P. Hier and   *Surveillance: Power, Problems, and*
Joshua Greenberg,   *Politics.* Vancouver, Canada:
eds.   University of British Columbia Press,
                      2009.

Susan Landau   *Surveillance or Security? The Risks*
                      Posed by New Wiretapping
                      Technologies. Cambridge, MA: MIT
                      Press, 2013.

Armand Matteralt   *The Globalization of Surveillance.*
                      Cambridge, MA: Polity Press, 2010.

Christian Parenti   *The Soft Cage: Surveillance in*
                      America from Slavery to the War on
                      Terror. Cambridge, MA: Basic Books,
                      2004.

Periodicals and Internet Sources

Alex Abdo   "You May Have 'Nothing to Hide'
                      but You Still Have Something to
                      Fear," American Civil Liberties
                      Union, August 2, 2013. www.aclu.org.

Tami Abdollah   "Officers' Body Cameras Raise
                      Privacy Concerns," Yahoo News,
                      March 15, 2014. http://news
                      .yahoo.com.

American Civil Liberties Union   "The Surveillance-Industrial Complex: How the American Government Is Conscripting Businesses and Individuals in the Construction of a Surveillance Society," 2004. www.aclu.org.

American Civil Liberties Union   "Time to Rein in the Surveillance State," 2014. www.aclu.org.

Stuart Armstrong   "Life in the Fishbowl," *Aeon*, September 30, 2013.

Associated Press   "Edward Snowden at SXSW Conference: I Saw the Constitution Being Violated on 'Massive Scale,'" March 11, 2014. www.nbcdfw.com.

Neal Augenstein   "National License Plate Database Sparks Privacy Fears," WTOP, February 17, 2014. www.wtop.com.

Peter Baker   "Obama's Path from Critic to Overseer of Spying," *New York Times*, January 15, 2014.

James Ball   "NSA and GCHQ Target 'Leaky' Phone Apps Like Angry Birds to Scoop User Data," *Guardian*, January 27, 2014.

Nick Bilton   "The Pros and Cons of a Surveillance Society," *New York Times* blog, July 16, 2013. http://bits.blogs.nytimes.com.

The Blaze   "Domestic Surveillance," 2014. www.theblaze.org.

| Darwin BondGraham and Ali Winston | "The Real Purpose of Oakland's Surveillance Center," *East Bay Express*, December 18, 2013. |

Danah Boyd | "The Problem with the 'I Have Nothing to Hide' Argument," *Dallas Morning News*, June 14, 2013.

David Brin | "World Cyberwar and the Inevitability of Radical Transparency," Metroactive, July 6, 2011. www.metroactive.com.

Zoë Carpenter | "What Obama Didn't Say in His Speech on NSA Spying," *Nation*, January 17, 2014.

Bill Chappell | "U.S. Agencies, Tech Firms Agree to Rules on Surveillance Info," National Public Radio, January 27, 2014. www.npr.org.

Jessica Chasmar | "L.A. Sheriff Admits to Testing Flyover Spy Program Without Notifying Residents," *Washington Times*, April 23, 2014.

Kyle Chayka | "Face-Recognition Software: Is This the End of Anonymity for All of Us?," *Independent*, April 23, 2014.

Danielle Keats Citron and David Gray | "Addressing the Harm of Total Surveillance: A Reply to Professor Neil Richards," *Harvard Law Review*, May 2013.

Liat Clark | "Get Ready to Have Your Biometrics Tracked 24/7," *Wired*, March 26, 2014.

Richard A. Clarke et al.   "Liberty and Security in a Changing World—Report and Recommendations of the President's Review Group on Intelligence and Communications Technologies," The White House, December 12, 2013. www.whitehouse.gov.

Stephanie Clifford and Quentin Hardy   "Attention, Shoppers: Store Is Tracking Your Cell," *New York Times*, July 14, 2013.

Sean Cockerham   "Some in Congress See Just One Option for NSA Spying: Scrap It," McClatchy, February 4, 2014. www.mcclatchydc.com.

Andrew Cohen   "Is the NSA's Spying Constitutional? It Depends Which Judge You Ask," *Atlantic*, December 27, 2013.

Tom Cohen, Jim Acosta, and Mariano Castillo   "Despite Obama's NSA Changes, Phone Records Still Collected," CNN, January 17, 2014. www.cnn.com.

Catherine Crump   "You Are Being Tracked—How License Plate Readers Are Being Used to Record Americans' Movements," American Civil Liberties Union, July 2013. www.aclu.org.

Democracy Now!   "Domestic Surveillance," 2014. www.democracynow.org.

Stephen Dinan and Ben Wolfgang   "Congress Split Over NSA's Domestic Spying Program, Could Just Let Laws Expire," *Washington Times*, January 19, 2014.

Charles Duhigg	"Psst, You in Aisle 5," *New York Times*, February 19, 2012.
Electronic Frontier Foundation	"Timeline of NSA Domestic Spying," 2014. www.eff.org.
Justin Elliott and Theodoric Meyer	"Claim on 'Attacks Thwarted' by NSA Spreads Despite Lack of Evidence," ProPublica, October 23, 2013. www.propublica.org.
Erica Fink	"This Drone Can Steal What's on Your Phone," CNN/Money, March 20, 2014. http://money.cnn.com.
Josh Gerstein	"Hillary Clinton Goes Mum on NSA, Skirts Surveillance Fight," *Politico*, February 17, 2014. www.politico.com.
Frida Ghitis	"U.S. Needs to Get Spying Under Control," CNN, October 25, 2013. www.cnn.com.
Amy Goodman and Denis Moynihan	"America's Real Subversives: FBI Spying Then, NSA Surveillance Now," *Democracy Now!*, July 25, 2013. www.democracynow.org.
Alan Greenblatt	"Our Surveillance Society: What Orwell and Kafka Might Say," National Public Radio, June 8, 2013. www.npr.org.
Glenn Greenwald	"Surveillance State Evils," *Salon*, April 21, 2012. www.salon.com.

Doug Gross   "Microsoft Fights Back Against NSA 'Snooping,'" CNN, December 9, 2013. www.cnn.com.

Doug Gross   "Anti-NSA Activists Don't Like Obama Speech," CNN, January 17, 2014. www.cnn.com.

Julian Hattem and Kate Tummarello   "Officials Defend NSA, Decry Snowden," *The Hill*, January 29, 2014. http://thehill.com.

Melanie Hicken   "Big Data Is Secretly Scoring You," CNN/Money, April 2, 2014. http://money.cnn.com.

Kashmir Hill   "Federal Judge Writes Epic Smackdown of 'Likely Unconstitutional' NSA Phone Record Collection," *Forbes*, December 16, 2013.

Michael Isikoff   "NSA Program Stopped No Terror Attacks, Says White House Panel Member," NBCNews, December 20, 2013. www.nbcnews.com.

Michael Isikoff   "After 43 Years, Activists Admit Theft at FBI Office that Exposed Domestic Spying," NBCNews, January 6, 2014. www.nbcnews.com.

Benny Johnson   "America's Spies Want Edward Snowden Dead," *BuzzFeed*, January 16, 2014. www.buzzfeed.com.

Amy Joyce   "Every Move You Make," *Washington Post*, October 1, 2006.

Heather Kelly

"Hobbyists Pilot Small Drones for Dogfights, Photography," CNN, January 24, 2014. www.cnn.com.

Arnold Kling

"David Brin's Transparent Society Revisited," Library of Economics and Liberty, July 1, 2013. www.econlib .org.

Richard Leon

"Memorandum Opinion, United States District Court for the District of Columbia," *Legal Times*, December 16, 2013.

Todd Lewan

"Microchips in Humans Spark Privacy Debate," *USA Today*, July 21, 2007.

Ashley Lutz and Matt Townsend

"Big Brother Is Watching You Shop," *Business Week*, December 15, 2011.

Katherine Mangu-Ward

"Don't Want the NSA to Read Your Documents? Use This Font," Reason.com, June 21, 2013. http://reason.com.

Kathleen Miller

"IRS Among Agencies Using License Plate-Tracking Vendor," Bloomberg, April 16, 2014. www.bloomberg.com.

Ellen Nakashima

"U.S. Reasserts Need to Keep Domestic Surveillance Secret," *Washington Post*, December 21, 2013.

Steven Nelson

"Snowden Says 'Many Other' Spy Programs Remain Secret, for Now," *US News & World Report*, March 7, 2014.

Scott Neuman — "The Case Against Clemency: Expert Says Snowden's Leaks Hurt Security," National Public Radio, January 9, 2014. www.npr.org.

New York Post — "Judge Says NSA Working to Save American Lives Within the Law, Rejects ACLU Lawsuit," December 27, 2013.

Ed O'Keefe — "Dianne Feinstein, Saxby Chambliss Explain, Defend NSA Phone Records Program," *Washington Post*, June 6, 2013.

Michael Pearson — "What Obama Changed at the NSA: 5 Takeaways," CNN, January 17, 2014. www.cnn.com.

Evan Perez — "U.S. to Let Tech Companies Release More Surveillance Data," CNN, January 27, 2014. www.cnn.com.

Daniel B. Prieto — "Civil Liberties and National Security After 9/11: A CFR Working Paper," Council on Foreign Relations, February 2009. www.cfr.org.

Neil M. Richards — "The Dangers of Surveillance," *Harvard Law Review*, May 2013.

Eugene Robinson — "Domestic Surveillance a Betrayal of Our Values," mySanAntonio.com, December 17, 2013. www.mysanantonio.com.

Mike Rosenberg   "San Jose Police Could Tap into Volunteer Residents' Private Security Cameras Under New Proposal," *San Jose Mercury News*, January 23, 2014.

George Santayana   "History Repeated: The Dangers of Domestic Spying by Federal Law Enforcement," American Civil Liberties Union, 2007. www.aclu.org.

Adrian Short   "When Does Face Scanning Tip Over into the Full-Time Surveillance Society?," *Guardian*, November 5, 2013.

Natasha Singer   "Shoppers Who Can't Have Secrets," *New York Times*, May 1, 2010.

Natasha Singer   "Revelations by AOL Boss Raise Fears Over Privacy," *New York Times*, February 10, 2014.

Daniel J. Solove   "Why Privacy Matters Even if You Have 'Nothing to Hide,'" *Chronicle of Higher Education*, May 15, 2011.

Doug Stanglin   "Federal Judge: NSA Phone Surveillance Legal," *USA Today*, December 27, 2013.

Jay Stanley   "Persistent Aerial Surveillance: Do We Want To Go There, America?," American Civil Liberties Union, February 7, 2014. www.aclu.org.

Jay Stanley and
Catherine Crump
"Protecting Privacy from Drone Surveillance: Recommendations for Governmental Use of Drone Aircraft," American Civil Liberties Union, December 2011. www.aclu.org.

Bruce Stokes
"NSA Spying: A Threat to US Interests?," *YaleGlobal*, December 5, 2013. http://yaleglobal.yale.edu.

Geoffrey R. Stone
"The NSA's Telephone Metadata Program Is Unconstitutional," *Huffington Post*, January 9, 2014. www.huffingtonpost.com.

Randall Stross
"Wearing a Badge, and a Video Camera," *New York Times*, April 6, 2013.

Gavin P. Sullivan
"Big Brother's Tracking Shines Light on Emerging Facial Recognition Technology," *Forbes*, July 9, 2013.

Craig Timberg
"New Surveillance Technology Can Track Everyone in an Area for Several Hours at a Time," *Washington Post*, February 5, 2014.

Craig Timberg
and Ashkan
Soltani
"By Cracking Cellphone Code, NSA Has Capacity for Decoding Private Conversations," *Washington Post*, December 13, 2013.

Time
"The Surveillance Society," accessed May 1, 2014. http://nation.time.com /surveillance-society.

Trevor Timm   "President Obama Claims the NSA
                     Has Never Abused Its Authority.
                     That's False," *Guardian*, December 31,
                     2013.

Alec Torres   "Tenn. State University Requires
                     Students to Wear Trackable IDs,"
                     National Review, February 28, 2014.

Mario Trujillo   "Paul on NSA Data: 'It Is Not About
                     Who Holds It,'" *The Hill*, January 17,
                     2014. http://thehill.com.

US Department   "Administration White Paper: Bulk
of Justice   Collection of Telephony Metadata
                     Under Section 215 of the USA
                     PATRIOT Act," August 9, 2013.
                     https://publicintelligence.net.

Matt Vespa   "NSA Official: 'We Are Now a Police
                     State,'" Christian News Service,
                     December 19, 2013. www.cnsnews
                     .com.

James Vlahos   "Surveillance Society: New High-Tech
                     Cameras Are Watching You," *Popular
                     Mechanics*, October 1, 2009.

David Von Drehle "The Surveillance Society," *Time*,
                     August 1, 2013.

Wall   "What They Know," accessed May 1,
Street Journal   2014. http://online.wsj.com
                     /public/page/what-they-know
                     -digital-privacy.html.

Washington Times "Total Surveillance Society," June 10,
                     2013.

David Welna   "What's the NSA Doing Now?
                     Training More Cyberwarriors,"
                     National Public Radio, April 30,
                     2014. www.npr.org.

Mark White   "Online Privacy: 'Big Data' Is
                     Watching, and Building Your Digital
                     Profile," *Sydney Morning Herald*,
                     January 18, 2014.

Index

D

E

F